HARDPRESS.NET
HOME OF HARD-TO-FIND BOOKS

The Turkish Slave, Or, the Dumb Dwarf of Constantinople
by Maturin Murray Ballou

Address:
HardPress
8345 NW 66TH ST #2561
MIAMI FL 33166-2626
USA
Email: info@hardpress.net

TEN CENT NOVELETTES.

THE TURKISH SLAVE, OR THE DUMB DWARF of CONSTANTINOPLE, BY LIEUT. MURRAY, COMPLETE. PRICE 10 Cts.

STANDARD AMERICAN AUTHORS

ELLIOTT, THOMES & TALBOT,
63 Congress St., Boston.

ELLIOTT, THOMES & TALBOT, Publishers
63 Congress Street, ...

THE

TURKISH SLAVE:

—OR,—

ᵗʰe Dumb Dwarf of Constantinoᵖ

A STORY OF THE EASTERN WORLD.

BY LIEUTENANT MURRAY.

BOSTON:
ELLIOTT, THOMES & TALBOT,
63 CONGRESS STREET.

THE TURKISH SLAVE.

CHAPTER I.

CITY OF CONSTANTINE.—THE BOSPHORUS.

CONSTANTINOPLE! what a crowd of oriental images throng before the mind's eye at the very mention of this capital of the indolent East. Unlike the olden cities of Europe, this gem of the Orient is not most interesting from historical lore, and the records of the past, but is still a vivid and living picture of all that fires the imagination, and delights the eye of the traveller. How peculiar are its people, made up of the quiet Armenian, the crafty, trading Jew, and the haughty Mussulman, with a sprinkling of Arabs from the desert, and slaves from the far East. And all these, with their varied and picturesque costumes, their indolent and dissipated habits, their luxurious mode of living, and their mysterious devotedness to the romantic creed of Mahomet.

Fair and beautiful, too, in itself is this unequalled emporium of the East, with its hundreds of mosques, capped with golden minarets, rising in lofty and delicate beauty towards the blue vault of heaven; its seraglio gardens, its closely guarded harems, its many and luxuriant fountains, its costly bazaars, thronged with the accumulated riches of the East, and, above all, its matchless Bosphorus, Golden Horn, and Valley of Sweet Waters —forming a constellation of local beauties and charms, that confound the traveller by their gorgeousness and number. No fairy tale hath yet rivalled the beauties of Constantinople, no imagination exceeded its luxuriant elegance. Here, gentle reader, in this city of Constantinople, this fairest capital of the Mahomets, does our story commence.

The golden light of the western sky was gilding the lofty spires of St. Sophia, as the sun set behind the horizon, when a young horseman dashed down the projecting point of land that makes out from Stamboul towards Asia, known as Seraglio Point. At a signal from the rider, a heavy portal was opened, and he rode within the walls that surround the royal grounds and palaces. What a proud home for a monarch was this! What a gem of beauty, cut off from the rest of the city by high walls, flanked by towers, and embracing a circuit of a league, crowded with varied and beautiful foliage, dark and lofty cypresses, gilded cupolas, gay balconies, and glittering domes. All these were lit up at this twilight hour in a dreamy hue, by the soft light that came daintily across the silvery sea of Marmora, when the palace gate opened, and the horseman before referred to passed within the sacred walls of the Seraglio.

The young horseman was evidently a Greek by his dress and bearing, but though he wore no turban of distinction, and bestrode his spirited Arab with a thoughtless yet easy grace, still the household guard saluted him profoundly, as he passed them and dashed up the noble avenues like one accustomed to the luxuriance and beauty about him. His dress was of the picturesque style of his nation, and his skull-cap of crimson velvet, with its heavy tassel of gold, set off to perfection the raven locks of the wearer. Picture to yourself a clear, high forehead, large black eyes, with lashes that should have belonged to a female, a classical formation of features, with a mouth almost effeminately beautiful, relieved by the faint line of a dark, silky moustache; add a figure slightly below the ordinary stature, and yet somewhat undeveloped, and you have the likeness of the young Greek, as he rode within the precincts of the sultan's palace.

The high-bred charger stood as though he had been riveted to the spot, when his rider, alighting, tossed the rein loose over his arching neck, pausing for a moment, to smooth with his hand the soft gloss of the beautiful animal's hide. Those who have never seen a true Arabian horse, can hardly conceive the beauty of such an animal—almost human in instinct, affectionate and docile as a child, proud and graceful in action, and as fleet as the wind! The Turk may *like* a favorite wife, but he *loves* his horse; he tends him constantly, feeds him with his own hands, talks to him, fondles him, lies by his side; or, mounting him, skims the desert like a bird upon the wing. The finest animal in the world, believe us, is a full-blooded Arabian horse.

In his quick, light, bounding action, scarce touching the ground, so proudly he prances—with delicate limbs, small-veined head, and fiery nostrils—a finely-rounded body, trembling with restrained and impatient energy—a curving and haughty neck, with a black and flowing mane—who can blame his master for esteeming his Arabian as something almost human, and for loving him as though he were his own flesh and blood? It was thus that the horseman felt as he looked upon the proud animal that had just carried him so bravely through a half dozen leagues over the soft green carpet of the Valley of Sweet Waters, from whence he had just returned.

As the Greek turned to enter the royal hall, he encountered, by the side of the portal, a being which at first glance seemed to be not more than half human. With the body of a man, it was yet so deformed and ugly as to be painful to look upon. A large hump was on its back, throwing the spine most awkwardly awry, one limb was much shorter than the other, and the arms were of remarkable length; add to these proportions, a face wrinkled and most singularly small, and a body dwarfed in development, and you have the semblance of the strange creature that stood by the sultan's portal. The only thing about the dwarf that was not repulsive, were his eyes, and these beamed upon the Greek with such a plaintive and gentle look, that a charm seemed to go with them, and he laid his hand kindly upon the poor deformed creature's head.

The dwarf was dumb, but he held a cinnamon rose towards the Greek, which the latter received with tokens of pleasure, and thrust quickly into his bosom, while he bestowed a handful of sweetmeats upon the dwarf, that he had just brought from the bazaars, in the city, and with a gentle pat upon the strangely deformed creature's shoulder, and nodding kindly to him, he went in. The dwarf thrust the sweetmeats unheeded into a fold of his dress, but the token of kindness that the Greek had bestowed upon him, was evidently working in his poor brain, as he rubbed his long skinny hands cheerfully together, and his bright, clear eyes followed the receding steps of the new comer. Then turning away, the dwarf hobbled round a clump of cypress trees, using, at every other step, his hands, as well as his feet, in walking.

The Greek, in the meantime, had entered the palace, receiving a pair of satin slippers from a slave at the door, in place of his boots, and now stood in the presence of the Sultan Mahomet, before whom he bowed low, in the style of the East.

"Alick!" said the sultan, removing for a moment the amber mouth-piece of his pipe from his lips to address his page, for that was the post that the young Greek filled so near his presence.

"Highness!" responded the page, bowing with profound respect.

"Were those Circassians purchased, as I directed, from the market to-day?"

"Highness, yes."

"And the two Georgians, that Brumah spoke to us about?"

"Highness, yes."

"And are they in charge of our chief eunuch within the wall?"

"Highness, yes," still assented the page.

"Did you satisfy the demand of the merchant?" continued the sultan.

"Highness, to the uttermost charge," replied the Greek.

"You are a faithful servant, Alick, and my commands never tarry in your keeping."

"Highness, my only duty is to serve you faithfully."

"God is great!" uttered the sultan, smoothing his beard in token of approval, and again resuming the inhalation of his perfumed tobacco, the exhilarating effect of which showed that of its component parts, opium formed not a small portion.

The page bowed low, and seeing by his master's expression that he would be left alone, to enjoy the wild, dreamy mood induced by the continued exhalation of the favorite drug, passed out at a side door of the grand hall, and left the Turkish monarch alone.

The young Greek stepped into a deep alcove opening upon a projected balcony, that commanded a lovely view of the surrounding scenery. The alcove was half hidden by the profusion of satins and Canton silks that formed the curtains, but throwing himself listlessly upon the soft velvet divans that covered the floor, he rested upon one arm, and looked out upon the lovely prospect afforded by the rising moon, as it poured its mellow light so prodigally along the Bosphorus and the valley of the Golden Horn. It was a sight to make poetry in the soul of an anchorite, and the page seemed to gaze with his very soul, while he hummed an air of his native land. At this moment a step approached him so lightly, and at a moment when he was so much absorbed, that he did not hear it until it stopped by his very side.

"Esmah!" exclaimed the page, in accents of undisguised pleasure, as he suddenly sprang to his feet, and confronted the new comer

"Alick!" responded a soft, silvery voice, from beneath a veil that seemed to lend a loveliness to the wearer's face, by only half concealing it, while the large, dreamy eyes that were bent so tenderly upon the page, told the observer, in language not to be misconstrued, that they were those of a lovely Circassian.

"How are you at liberty at this hour, Esmah?" asked the page, gently.

"In coming from the bath, I hid in the hall of fountains, and came on after the rest had passed into the gates of the harem."

"But they will discover thee, and blame this conduct, Esmah."

"I have no fear."

"No fear, Esmah?"

"None!"

"Suspicion is enough to condemn thee, Esmah. Dost not remember the two Georgians that were drowned in the Bosphorus, within this month, on mere suspicion?"

"True; and a faithful slave was sacrificed at the same time, as a party in the sin."

"As innocent, doubtless, of wrong as ourselves, Esmah," said the page.

"True, Alick; but they are better off now," said the gentle girl, sighing.

"God forgive their murderers!" said the Greek sternly, and with a flashing eye, for the spirit of his nation burnt clear and bright in his young breast.

"It makes me tremble, Alick, to see thee look thus," said the gentle girl.

"Nay, you need not fear, Esmah; you would turn the boldest thoughts to love."

Taking the hand of the young and beautiful creature by his side, the page led her still nearer to the balcony, and pointed, with inspiration in his look, to the splendid scenery that opened before them. There lay the city, so quiet, that it seemed as if asleep; the moon danced with silvery light upon the star-shaped bay and among the gilded caiques, while the sultan's fleet rode there, with their blood-red flags flaunting in the night-breeze. There lay the seven hills of ancient Stamboul, and a hundred gold-tipped minarets coquetting with the light, and the whole course of the Bosphorus, from Marmora to the Black Sea, hedged in on either side by imperial palaces, valleys, hills, and mosques! How truly oriental was the picture!

"Beautiful!" whispered Esmah, leaning more closely upon the page's arm, as she gazed delightedly on the scene.

"Its beauties are all enhanced to me by sharing them with thee," said the page, tenderly.

"You seem never tired of watching this scenery, Alick. How often have I found thee in this very spot," she said, looking deep into his soul-lit eyes with her own dreamy orbs.

"Dearest, it is our trysting-place; but you, too, enjoy such a scene as this?"

"Ah, yes, since you have taught me so much, Alick; but I have seen these things from a child, and thought little of them, until seen with thee," said the fair girl, innocently.

"Dear Esmah," he answered, placing both her hands upon his breast; and holding them there, he looked tenderly into her languid and beautiful eyes. "I fear that even what little I have taught thee will serve to render thee more miserable."

"Impossible, Alick!" interrupted Esmah. "How is such a result possible, when I feel every hour that you have opened to me new scenes of enjoyment, that else were all unheeded?"

"Nay, dearest, I fear that it may do so, by awakening within thy breast a realizing sense of thy true position. But I have loved thee so well, that I could not but speak out my whole soul to thee," continued the page, pressing still more nearly the soft hands he held to his heart. "I have known no happiness unless shared with thee."

"Dear Alick," whispered the maiden, "all you have done is for the best; you could not do wrong with such noble principles to guide, as those which actuate your heart."

"In your kind consideration, Esmah, you make far too much of my poor deserts," said the page.

"Not so, Alick," she replied. "I have studied too earnestly your disposition and character, not to speak truly of them."

"Dearest!" he murmured, pressing again more tenderly the hands he held.

Esmah's eyes were even more eloquent than words! And the page stood there like one entranced, drinking from the depth of their purity, and forgetting all else but her loveliness and the love she bore for him. Few such moments may occur in a life time, and he realized that, scarcely wishing to break the soft spell that bound them, by action or words.

"Hark!" said the page, starting and listening to catch some faint sound of footsteps, that he fancied to have heard approaching the spot where they stood.

"It ⬤Brumah's step—I know it well," said Esmah. "He comes to conduct me back to the harem; but I must not be seen with you, Alick—what is to be done?"

"No, that were fatal indeed," said the page, quickly, looking about him.

"Where can you hide?"

"Behind the curtain, or else I will out at the window; but stay, let me make sure that he comes this way first."

"If aught should befall thee, Alick, I should never forgive my—"

"It is indeed he."

"Quick, for your life!"

"I will outwit him."

"Farewell, then. Pray, go!"

"Stay," said the page, quickly impressing a kiss upon her hand; and in another moment he had swung himself lightly from his balcony to the green sward of the seraglio garden beneath, leaving Esmah to be conducted back to the sultan's cage for his birds, as he called his harem, by Brumah, the chief of the eunuchs, an important officer in the household service of a sultan.

CHAPTER II.

THE STAR OF THE HAREM.

In a land where personal beauty alone makes the market value for a woman, and where the main occupation is bathing, eating and administering to the amusement of their Turkish masters, or engaging in sentimental correspondence, by means of flowers, with the forbidden Greeks and Armenians, it is not to be supposed that there is any great degree of intelligence to be found among the gentle sex, and therefore, when, by any strange chance, such a phenomenon as a woman evincing any tokens of a cultivated mind appeared in Constantinople, it was deemed and treated as something quite remarkable. Unlike her sex in any other part of the world, Nature seems to have made the woman of the East, though noted for their sentiment of character, yet mere toys; beautiful, indolent, childlike creatures.

Beautiful as the most beautiful, yet evincing a rare cultivation of mind and refinement of taste, Esmah, daughter of the Grand Sultan Mahomet, by his favorite Circassian wife, was the star of her father's palace. Though but sixteen years of age, she was said to possess more influence over the proud and austere. monarch, her father, than his entire court could boast. From her very infancy, he had loved and doted upon her with a most un-mussulmanlike fondness, and as she grew up in womanly beauty, and showed signs of remarkable mental ability, the father was more proud of her than any of his most promising sons, even those that were nearest to his succession. In short, Esmah realized Moore's beautiful picture:

> " But never yet hath bride or maid,
>   In Araby's gay harems smiled,
>   Whose boasted brightness would not fade
>   Before Al Hassan's blooming child."

The austere old Turk would sit by her side, and talk or smoke with a satisfaction that left him in most generous and agreeable good spirits, and on such occasions he would, when well satisfied with himself and all the world, when a dreamy, half intoxicated influence pervaded his brain, call in his page Alick, to sing and play to him upon his guitar. The Greek was a natural musician, and his wild, free touch, and the plaintive national lays that he chanted were so thrilling and spirited, and then so soft and winning, that they never tired but rather won the heart of the listener, more and more. And finally, when the sultan was overcome by the opium, which, perhaps, Alick would sometimes put in his pipe rather largely, then Esmah would steal away from her father's side to that of the young Greek, and thus were many golden hours passed in interchange of thought and feeling between the Princess Esmah and the sultan's humble page. They were young, thoughtless, and almost too happy thus together, in a spot sacred from all intrusion.

" Now tell me one of those stories that I like so well, but which you never repeat in my father's waking hours," Esmah would say.

"And do you like them so well then?" asked the page tenderly.

" O, beyond everything," she would reply, with an innocent and earnest look.

" I could sit and tell them to thee forever."

" And I could ever listen."

"Ah! dear one," said the page, " I would that you were humble like myself, and that we had met in my native land, of which I so often tell thee; we would have been so happy there; all the world to each other, and no fear to mar our joy, no rank to separate us. Dost remember the tale I told thee yesterday, as we sat here, Esmah?"

" I do indeed, Alick; 'twas of an humble maid, and as humble a lover, who, though poor, almost to very penury, yet loved so dearly, were so true and faithful to each other, that they heeded not the frowns of fortune until a good spirit, whose charge it was to watch over virtue and humble merit, showed to the lover in a dream a mine of gold; awakening from the slumber, the lover sought and found the goodly wealth he dreamed of, but fearing to tempt a heart now so pure and good, when the youth had got enough of the gold for comfortable subsistence, he dreamed again, and was made by the spirit to forget the spot, which ever after he could not find. But his fidelity was rewarded, and they were happy."

" You remember well, dearest," said the page. " Now would I that we were that humble couple, with not enough of riches to make us luxuriant, and yet enough to be beyond the reach of want, and thus in humble life our lot was cast. Could not you be happy thus, Esmah?"

" Happy? yes! beyond comparison blessed, Alick, could that humble lot be shared with thee?"

"Ah, dearest girl, these are but pictures and vain fancies; for fate, hard fate, hath separated us by iron bonds!"

" Not irrevocably, Alick."

" We can only hope that is the case, Esmah—but in the face of plain, straight-forward reason, I can read but little hope."

" Alas! how sad you are to-day," said the princess, sighing.

" Nay, am I sad? I would not be so before thee, dear one."

" Then talk no more of this, but tell me again of your native land, and picture it to me as you have always done, for already I feel as though it were my own, so well I love it."

"It is a pleasant task, Esmah—pleasant to talk of beloved Greece, and sweet to have thee for a listener."

At such moments he told her, with thrilling eloquence, of his native land, and instilled into her heart self-respect and a love of virtue. He taught her the true dignity of her sex, and how woman was esteemed and cherished in other countries.

He filled her young and impressible mind with the fire and freedom of patriotism, told her a hundred old legends of chivalry and love, that he had learned in boyhood, and taught her to read and compose, qualifications deemed quite superfluous in a Turkish harem. Thus, step by step, and day by day, the young Greek grew in the affections of the princess, until Esmah loved him beyond all else in life, giving him her whole heart, and centering all her hopes in him, who was so far below her in position that she could never hope to call him husband. Such an idea was in contradiction to all her experience and knowledge, and she knew that her love, publicly acknowledged, would be a criminal offence in Constantinople.

But we must return to the page, who did not so easily get rid of the consequences of their last meeting in the alcove of the balcony. We left Alick just as he had swung himself from the balcony window to the ground, after kissing Esmah's hand. Scarcely had he recovered himself upon his feet, when an officer of the household, on duty near the spot, rudely seized him by the arm, exclaiming at the same time:

"Dog of a Christian, thou hast polluted the princess with a kiss! It was witnessed, and thou must die to expiate the sin. Come before the sultan, that he may adjudge thee to the bow-string at once, as thou richly deservest. The curse of Allah rest upon thy head!"

"Loose thy hold!" said the page, while his dark eye flashed with anger.

"Never!" replied the Turk, grasping him still more fiercely.

"Wilt unloose me?" repeated the Greek, struggling with his stronger antagonist.

"By the prophet, no!" growled forth the Turk, as he drew a pistol from his belt and directed it towards Alick's breast.

The page hesitated no longer. He knew but too well the Turkish character; he knew that the two most sacred things to a Mahometan were his grave and his harem, and that, however kind the sultan had been to him heretofore, if he should appear before him thus accused, his fate would be inevitable, and he must die; and, indeed, that if the law was strictly enforced, as it regarded both parties, Esmah would be placed in a sack and sunk to the bottom of the Bosphorus before the setting of another sun. We say the page realized all this, but it was by one single comprehensive thought, such as crosses the mind when we are placed in any remarkable and important position. That which occupies so much space and time in description, was like an electric spark in the page's brain. His mind was made up in a moment—the witness of the liberty he had taken must die! And in the next instant the bright stiletto of the page gleamed in the moonbeams, as it was raised to strike. But it was a wily man he had to contend with, one who had been a soldier in the wars, and whose hand and eye were trained for every emergency, and with a blow as quick as his own motion, the Turk dashed the glittering weapon to the ground by a stroke from his pistol, still pressing on with his prisoner to the point where the main guard were posted. A few steps more and they would turn the angle of the palace wall, and be in full sight of the main guard. The corner once passed, and Alick felt that his sacrifice was certain. The thought seemed to give him renewed strength, and he struggled fiercely with his captor, who yet held him in his iron grasp. Suddenly, in the struggle, the Turk uttered a deep moan, that seemed scarcely to escape his lips, turned with his face towards Mecca, the tomb of the prophet, and fell without a cry upon the silken greensward of the seraglio—a corpse!

It was all done so silently, so quickly, so like a miracle, that the page stood like one confounded, neither turning to the right nor the left, but gazing still upon the lifeless form of the Mussulman, until an arm was laid upon his own, and he was drawn away from the spot, almost forcibly, by the dwarf, who, as he coolly wiped the page's dagger, which he had picked up and used so effectually, made a motion for Alick to fly into the palace before the body was discovered, while he leaped away towards a clump of cypresses, one of which he clambered like a monkey, and sat watching the deed he had done from among the thick branches.

Leaving this dumb and singular witness to watch the lifeless body of the Turk, as the limbs stiffened in the night dew, we must ask the reader to go back a few years with us in the thread of our story, that he may become the better acquainted with some of the characters destined to enact an important part in the story that we relate.

It was some eight years before the period at which our story opens, one clear, autumnal day, that the Sultan Mahomet and his court visited the royal mosque in state, to commemorate some high occasion in the annals of the church. The sultan's caique, or boat, with its fifty oarsmen, was returning across the harbor after the hour of devotion, the guns of the Turkish fleet had thundered forth their royal salute, the yards had been manned, and the colors hoisted and lowered, in due token of the royal presence, and the boat itself was quietly shooting through the water, when a little female child, leaning observantly from the window of the caique, became startled by the flapping of one of the gay streamers of the boat in her very face, and springing forward, it fell into the sea!

At the moment of the accident the sultan's barge was passing under the quarter of a Trebizond slaver, in the shrouds of which a small lad had placed himself, and from whence he was intently watching the gay display upon the waters of the harbor, and the progress of the royal cortege. His quick eye was the first to observe the accident to the child, and scarcely had the caique shot three times its own length by the spot, propelled by the many oars that forced it on, before he had dashed into the tide, and was already supporting the child with one hand, while he struck boldly out with the other in pursuit of the royal barge, which was now stationary.

It is not often that your true Turk, your full blooded Mussulman, is discomposed from his dignity and calm expression of fatality, even for a moment. Like the North American Indian, he permits nothing to surprise or in the least disconcert him. But the sight of the brave boy, scarcely older than the child that had so nearly perished, thus bravely and stoutly supporting her, drew from the Mahometan boat crew one spontaneous and wild shout of excitement, that made the frail caique tremble in every inch of its make. Even the proud and imperial master, who held the lives of millions at his beck and order, turned aside now, while the feelings of the man predominated, to dash away a tear as the two were taken in over the side.

Scarcely had the brave boy given up his charge on board the sultan's caique into the very arms of the monarch himself, when a boat from the slaver came alongside, and the captain coolly demanded possession of the boy who had performed the noble act.

" Is he thy boy ?" asked the sultan of the captain.

"He is my slave," replied the master of the Trebizond ship, as he bowed low in the eastern style before the Sultan Mahomet.

"From whence do you come?" continued the sultan.

"From the south, highness," replied the slaver, again bowing low.

"And this boy?"

"Is a Greek."

"And from whence?"

"He was taken from the fishermen of the Archipelago, highness," replied the man.

"'Tis well. God is good, and the law is sacred. Take thy property," said the sultan.

"Highness, I kiss your hand," replied the captain, bowing to the thwarts of his boat.

At this moment there struggled through the crowd a strangely-deformed creature, and seizing the boy, he looked strangely into his face for a moment, and placing a ring upon his finger again disappeared within the curtains of the boat. Hardly understanding this singular gift, the boy seemed to be pleased with the ring, which was one of rare workmanship, in gold, supporting a small diamond of surpassing brilliancy. The boy had marked the giver, who seemed to be a privileged person in the sultan's barge, though deformed and horrible to look upon.

In the meantime the sultan turned to the cushions of his caique, to attend to the half-drowned child that had been so providentially rescued from a watery grave. The boy returned at once to the slaver with his master, thinking lightly of what he had done. The royal boat swept on to the Seraglio Point, and in a couple of hours the whole affair was forgotten, or at least apparently so, among a people who are stoics both by practice and by nature, and who die or live, as the fates may decree, without a murmur, or even a thought that by any possible act of their own they might in any way avert the decree of fortune. They are devotedly and sincerely fatalists, and live up to the dictates of their belief most religiously.

What seaman, who has sailed in the Black Sea, or among the isles of the Grecian Archipelago, has not seen these Turks calmly resign themselves and their well-found crafts to the mercy of a wild storm, and lighting a pipe, sit down contentedly on the deck to await the fate that is ordained for them, saying, "If we are to die, no effort of ours can avail us; if we are to be saved, we shall be so without any agency of our own. Allah needs

not the aid of such as we to carry out his will What availeth
our exertions ?"

Far be it from us to disparage entire reliance upon Divine
Providence, more especially in time of imminent danger; but a
storm at sea calls for a cool head and a prompt spirit on the
quarter-deck, with ready activity to back them on the forecastle.
Resignation is a very good spirit to possess, but a worthless
servant.

CHAPTER III.

SLAVE MARKET OF CONSTANTINOPLE.

IT was just one week subsequent to the accident that had occurred on board the sultan's caique, in the harbor of Constantinople, that a public sale of the cargo of slaves brought by the
Trebizond ship took place in the bazaar. A curious scene was
presented, with its group of males and females, to be bargained for
and sold like so many cattle.   There were rosy-cheeked Circassian girls and boys, stout, manly Greeks, captured- from their
fishing-boats in the Ægean Sea, Persians Georgians, the latter
mostly young and beautiful girls, brought expressly to grace the
harems of the rich and noble Mussulmans, each one destined to
be the plaything of some " malignant and turbaned Turk."

At one corner of the bazaar there stood quietly by himself, a
small boy, of some twelve or thirteen summers, dressed in the
fisherman's costume of the Greeks of Negropont. The most
casual observer might easily perceive that he was no common
boy. His active eye took in every movement of the crowd, and
all that transpired in the thronged bazaar. He was quick, observant, thoughtful and handsome. His light form displayed
flexibility of limb and strength of body, well combined, and the
feat in the harbor showed his promptness and daring, for it was
he who had saved the child that fell from the sultan's caique
but a few days before.

A perfume merchant had set his eyes upon the boy, as peculiarly adapted for his service in his bazaar, and a captain of the
sultan's guard had already resolved to purchase him, as a lackey
to tend his horse and trappings, while some half dozen others,

struck with his remarkable manner and appearance, had also made up their minds that he must be theirs.

"Wouldst like me for thy master, boy?" said the perfume merchant, accosting the young Greek.

The boy looked at him with a singular mixture of contempt and curiosity depicted in his face, and being attracted by some passing event, he heeded not the question that the man of perfumes had made.

"Wouldst like me for a master, boy?" repeated the Turk.

"You *smell* well," said the boy, with a quick, sarcastic wit, that raised a shout of laughter among the mixed assembly.

The merchant turned away, resolving to buy him, if only for the pleasure of revenging himself for the insult of the young rogue. The captain of the cavalry, having marked the scene between the boy and the perfume merchant, liked him all the better for his wit and spirit, and approaching him said:

"I'm a soldier, my lad—how would you like to be my page, and have the care of my horses' trappings?"

"I care not to whom I'm sold," said the boy, listlessly.

"But you should, my little fellow. It may make vast odds to you."

"Am I not a slave in any instance?" asked the young Greek, turning his fine eye upon the soldier with an expressive and meaning glance.

"In the name, thou art; but with a good master it is of little account."

"I care not," replied the boy, "whether my cage be barred with golden walls or iron; it is a cage all the same to me."

"I like thee, nevertheless," said the soldier, "and will try for thee."

The boy answered not further, but turned listlessly away to gaze at the scene that surrounded him in the slave bazaar, while his handsome face expressed many contending emotions, elicited by the doings there. He seemed utterly unconscious of the attention that was bestowed upon himself, and the general admiration that his appearance elicited from all.

Circassian after Circassian was "knocked down" to the highest bidder, stout Greeks and Bulgarian lads were sold at a bargain, intermingled with the beautiful Georgians, till the Greek fisher boy was offered at last to close the sale. He was announced by the Jew who acted as salesman, as a fisher boy from the Archipelago, and as an instance of his promptness and ability, his late service to the sultan was related. The boy stood with a proud and curling lip as he was offered there for sale, but remained passive and speechless. The bids ran high, and already the boy was going at a price far exceeding that of the highest Georgian, much to the delight and surprise of his owner, the captain of the slave ship, when the dwarf who placed the ring upon his finger hobbled into the bazaar, and hurrying to the side of one who wore the livery of the sultan's household, made a sign to him, and disappeared as suddenly as he had come.

In the next moment the well-known voice of Brumah, the sultan's chief eunuch, put a stop to the sale, by offering twice the sum that had been already bidden; and taking the boy by the hand, he laid a bag of gold on the owner's stand, and walked away with his purchase. It was thus that Alick the Greek was introduced into the palace of the sultan—and Esmah, the lovely princess, was the child whom he had saved from a grave in the waters of the Bosphorus.

Alick was too young to know much of his own history. He knew that he was born at Athens, that having lost both his parents while yet quite a child, an old priest had adopted him, with whom he had lived on the island of Negropont ever since. This he had been told an hundred times, in answer to his natural, childlike inquiries. The priest had never been a father, and with all his supposed knowledge of human nature, knew little of the proper way to educate or bring up a child, but he tutored him profoundly in such branches as were deep study even for himself. Thus, from his earliest childhood, the boy had begun to learn those things which are supposed to be within the compass only of maturer minds. This constant application and hard study had tended in some degree to affect the health of one so young as Alick, and the good priest, realizing this, had given him a few months' vacation; and to strengthen and develop his young frame, as well as to humor a natural taste that he seemed to possess for anything relating to the sea, he placed him in charge of a fisherman of the isle, who belonged to Negropont; and from this craft the boy had been taken by the piratical slaver, while on a fishing excursion off the isle of Scio.

Already greatly prepossessed in favor of Alick, the sultan kept him near his person, vastly entertained by his conversational powers, for his young mind was richly stored with tales and legends of his country, told to him by the priest, besides numberless Greek songs and ballads, which the boy would sing, accompanying himself upon the guitar which he played with skill, thanks to the undivided attention of his ghostly instructor. The sultan, appreciating his many excellent acquirements and intrepidity of character, made Alick his body page, and the young Greek grew up to be of the utmost importance to the comfort of his royal master, from the fact that his shrewdness had led him to make the sultan's wants his study, and had also taught him the art to please and serve him faithfully. Like Othello the Moor, he sat before Esmah and her father, and told his stories to the delight of their leisure hours, and winning the daughter's heart little by little, till it was all his own.

. "And did this old priest teach thee all these things?" the sultan would often ask, after listening delightedly to the boy's relation of some old romantic story.

"All, highness."

"But you must have been an apt pupil, Alick, to remember so well?"

"I loved to listen to them, highness, for I knew no other pleasure."

"And you were an orphan, Alick?" asked the monarch, sympathizingly.

"While yet almost an infant, highness," replied the page.

"And never knew a parent's care?" continued the sultan, whose sympathy was vastly promoted by the drug he was now inhaling.

"Never, highness, save that of the kind old priest who adopted me."

"Think of it, Esmah," the sultan would say, turning to his daughter, while she showed by the language of her eyes how *much* she thought of all that concerned the page.

"God is great—we will be a father to thee," the sultan would say, as his eyeballs gradually dilated under the narcotic influence of the strong potations of the dreamy drug, and visions of delight floated in his half-conscious imagination.

All the while, Esmah was regarding Alick with a tender but silent eloquence, that words would only have marred, and little did the Greek boy think of his servitude. Little did he realize, under such circumstances, that he was a slave!

Time flew with fairy-like wings for him. He heeded not its passage. Days, weeks, months, all unheeded, went into the lap of time, uncounted and unrecorded by him, for his heart was full and rich in contentment, so that he was but loved by Esmah,

and permitted, even thus in secret, to exchange those sweet·
promises and assurances that made them both so happy.   Who
could find fault with their intimacy?   They were scarcely
more than children, and there was such a native grace and
dignity in the manner of the Greek boy, that he seemed fully
the equal of Esmah in station, though his tongue and bearing
seemed so humble and dutiful.   Yes, they were sweet playmates,
and many an eye looked with envy upon the page, to see how
much the fair and youthful princess regarded and relied upon him
for amusements.

There were times, latterly, as Esmah grew up towards womanhood, that Brumah, the chief of the sultan's private household, looked with jealous eye upon the intimacy of the children,
and once or twice he had even ventured to separate them when
they were engaged in their games in the seraglio gardens, and
send Alick to some other part of the palace; but he did not often
take this liberty, for Esmah administered to him a reprimand
that cut him keenly, child as she was; and the chief eunuch
really feared the child, whom he knew to be so strong a favorite
with the sultan, that the monarch was easily swayed by her
will, upon any ordinary subject.   Therefore he took care to
offend her no further.

Time passed on, day by day.   Alick and Esmah were much
together, playing among the beautiful fountains and fragrant
flowers of the seraglio gardens.   They were but children, and
no one in that proud household regarded their intimacy, even
for a moment, in any other light than of childish mates.   Still
the intelligent young Greek knew the part he played too well
not to appear, more especially before others, to show the most·
profound respect towards her whom he already loved as a dear
sister.   Their young minds were moulded thus alike from childhood, by constant communion, and Alick, having imbibed a
taste for study, soon mastered her native tongue, and taught
her his own.   Indeed, the sultan seemed pleased at this, and
rewarded Alick for the instruction he imparted, with a diamond-
hilted stiletto of great value, containing a Damascus blade of
rare workmanship and unrivalled temper.   The sultan forgot,
that in Esmah's learning Alick's native tongue, the young
couple were enabled to converse upon any subject that they
chose, in a language to which himself and household were utter
strangers.

While Alick had instructed Esmah in his native language, he

had also taught her his religion, the Christian's faith, as it had
been impressed upon his mind daily, by the old priest of Negropont, and the young girl joined him often in tender and heart-
felt prayer. But O, how secretly! Had they been detected,
Alick knew full well that even the sultan's earnest friendship
would not save him from instant death by the bow-string.
Indeed, there were constant examples to this effect exhibited
almost daily before his eyes. Perhaps the very consciousness
of the danger that they shared in their religious sentiments, by
bowing the knee together in the Christian prayer, lent to the
ceremony additional force and interest.

Under these circumstances, it is no matter of surprise that
they grew to love each other so tenderly and devotedly. Esmah,
from contrasting the character of the females that surrounded
her with the picture of those which Alick had often drawn for
her, and from the representations of the respect in which her
sex was held by Christian nations, was led to look upon the
real homage that the Greek paid her as something actually sacred, and she loved him accordingly, with all the wealth and
devotedness of her pure soul.

"But O, how thoroughly hopeless is such love as ours, Esmah," said the young Greek, as they sat alone in a shaded alcove
one afternoon, after the sultan had dropped away, overcome by
his favorite drug, in dreamy bliss.

"Hopeless indeed," sighed Esmah.

"There are so many barriers to our union, that even love
cannot hope."

"Thy want of rank, Alick, is all, is it not?" she asked.

"Not all, dearest."

"Why not all, since I love thee, and thou lovest me, and my
father, too, loves thee well?"

"You forget one other reason," replied Alick, seriously.

"Ah, true—your religion; nay, *my* religion, Alick, for I, too,
am a Christian. But among the high and noble, even mixed
marriages have been tolerated by my father and his advisers,"
replied Esmah.

"Ay, perhaps an emperor might be sanctioned in a marriage
with thee; but not an humble personage—much less a page. I
could never consent to change my faith, even for thee, dearest,
and that alone would separate us in this country."

"Were you disposed to do so, Alick, I could not love you so
well as I now do; for I feel that the depth of my affection is

founded much upon your Christian character, your native honesty and truth," replied the thoughtful girl.

"Dear girl, you make me feel that I am unworthy of such love," said the page, expressing his honest feelings.

"Nay, Alick," said the gentle girl, drawing affectionately nearer to his side.

"But I speak honestly, dearest. Am I not the humblest of the humble, while you are the princess of the Sultan Mahomet, the proud master of the East?"

"You have levelled all barriers of birth, Alick, in opening to me the intellectual field that I should otherwise never have enjoyed. Your talent, and our happy faith, the true religion that you have taught me, levels all rank," said the princess, earnestly.

"Be this even so, Esmah, still how am I so worthy as thou art? What sacrifice do I make? None! I rise in seeking your love; you *come down* to me in accepting and returning it. What have you to gain? Nothing, save the true love of this poor heart. What to lose? Position, riches, splendor—everything!"

"Nay, Alick, you distress me by talking thus," said Esmah, earnestly.

"What are you, Esmah? A princess!"

"Alick, Alick!" interrupted the fair girl, holding up both her hands.

"Who am I? A slave!" continued the Greek, with bitterness.

Esmah started to her feet. It was not often that the word was uttered between them, and when she did hear it, it cut her to the very soul. She could not bear to think that he whom she loved, nay, almost adored, was her father's slave, bought with gold; ay, and liable to be sold again in the slave bazaar to-morrow. She covered her face with her hands as he spoke, and her soft, white bosom heaved audibly to the internal emotion that her struggling heart evinced.

One gentle pressure of her hand to his breast, one single assurance that, come what might, he should love her to the last, and with his whole soul, re-assured and calmed her, and they were happy again—happy in the present joy that each realized in the society of the other, and in shutting their eyes to the lowering darkness of the future. How hopeful is youth!

The most thoughtless reader will at once realize the imminent danger of the page's situation, even had he lived in a

Christian land, and dared to aspire to the love of one so vastly above him. But here, where the least intimacy between a Christian and the females of the Turks is regarded with the utmost jealousy, and when the sultan's displeasure, however trifling, amounts generally to instant death, without so much as a hearing on behalf of the victim, it will be seen that the young Greek was not unlike a man sleeping upon a mine of powder, that at any instant was liable to explode, and totally destroy him.

But we must on to more vivid and intricate portions of our story, where the reader may follow us with an awakening and increasing interest.

CHAPTER IV.

THE TURKISH SLAVE MASTER OF THE SULTAN'S YACHT.

WE left Alick just after he had escaped, by the dwarf's assistance, from the custody of the infidel, who was made to bite the dust by the well-directed blow from the page's dumb but faithful friend. With Alick's means of access to the sultan's palace, he was almost instantly by his royal master's side again, and apparently as unconcerned as before the late fatal business in which he had been engaged. A slight investigation of course followed the death of the Turk, and some witnesses were examined; but Alick would have been the last person on whom suspicion would rest, more especially as the dwarf, who was present at the examination of the subject, seemed to intimate by signs that he knew the murderer to be a Mussulman, and that he had escaped by the sea-wall of the seraglio in a boat on the Bosphorus.

This singular being, who has more than once been referred to in this story, was a privileged person about the court; indeed, he was looked upon with a sort of mysterious dread by most of the household, who attached some superstitious fear to his person, as do nearly all inhabitants of the East to deformity, of any character, evinced in the human species. This, however, was not the case with Esmah or Alick; both seemed to regard the dwarf only with the utmost kindness, and he—poor, deformed creature—probably loved them better than all else in the world for the spirit they had ever evinced towards him. He was born in the sultan's service, and possessed no small degree of importance, from the fact that such a person in a family is supposed by the Turks to prevent what they call the visit of the *evil eye*, a peculiar superstition of the East.

It so happened that Alick had once, by his intrepidity, and by great personal risk, saved the dwarf's life, at a time when one of the buildings where he was sleeping had become completely enveloped in flames. The dwarf had retreated to the upper part, and sat trembling with fear upon the very roof, not daring to approach the ordinary passages of egress, from the fact that they were already enveloped in flames. At this moment Alick rushed into the burning mass, and by almost superhuman exertion of strength, brought out the dwarf in his arms, though both were so severely burnt in their bodies as to suffer for a long time afterwards. Of course this caused the dwarf to regard Alick as his benefactor and best friend. Besides this, the page often served him in a manner that others would hardly have paused to consider.

The dwarf was permitted to roam where he pleased, and, having the most unbounded liberty within the royal apartments and the palace itself, was often the medium of messages from Esmah to Alick; and the reader will remember, in the opening of this story, of his presenting the page with a rose, which Alick thrust in his bosom with secret delight. The dwarf was possessed with a vast deal more intelligence than was generally accorded to him. He realized fully the situation of the page and Esmah; he knew that they loved each other, and he knew, too, how secretly and how hopelessly. They were the only two beings that the dwarf loved in the world; and he made them, and how he might serve and please them, his constant study.

They knew full well how devoted the poor creature was to them; but yet they knew not the extent and depth of that devotion, prompted by gratitude and love, in a heart peculiarly susceptible to these gentle influences, though fortune, in the outward make of the dwarf, had so belied all gentle sympathies. Esmah and Alick scarcely met together that he was not a silent and deaf watcher over them, unseen and unheeded. Like a faithful dog denied the power of expressing his affection, save by deeds, and by constant attendance and watchfulness, the poor dwarf could only thus manifest his warm affection for his young mistress and the page. Though naturally timid, because he could not understand the principle that moved things about him, yet, in their cause, he was brave to recklessness, and would not have hesitated to lay down his poor life in the defence of either. Poor dwarf! more human far than most of the world in thy disinterested devotedness, and the sincerity of thy humble love.

Sometimes, when Esmah resorted to the shade of the tall, proud cypresses, to read in the open air, the dwarf would creep to her feet, and, curling himself in a fold like an animal, lay his head by her side, and *seem* to sleep; while the princess would lay her soft, white hand upon his dark, wrinkled brow, and speak kindly, and smile upon him ever and anon. We say the poor, deformed creature *seemed* to sleep; but O, how wakeful was his heart!—how it throbbed at the kindness of the lovely girl, and how happy was the poor, lone dwarf beneath her smiles! They were a strange couple there together—so much loveliness and so much deformity! And when she left the spot, the dwarf would nestle down to where she had been sitting, as though she had left the dear influence of her presence still upon the place. Poor, devoted creature!

The Sultan Mahomet had early trusted the charge of his boats and yacht to his page, mainly because he had witnessed his intrepidity upon the water, and partly because he knew that Alick had both a taste for nautical matters and also some experience in them. Thus confided in, the Greek had so trained and disciplined the sultan's boat's crew to the state barge, as to astonish the seamen of the port, who at best are poor sailors. The sultan's elegant yacht having also been altered and improved in its sailing gear, after the English style, at the suggestion of Alick, he had got it in superb trim, and often delighted the sultan and his friends by his management, as they sailed upon the waters of Marmora. The boat was not more than ninety tons burthen, but was found in every elegance, comfort and necessity that the heart could desire; while Alick was permitted to pick his own crew, and to drill them after his own fashion.

The Golden Horn, as she was called, after that beautiful arm of the Bosphorus that seems to half embrace the city, was lugger-rigged, and carried a couple of guns of as heavy calibre as her tonnage would admit, besides a full supply of small arms and ammunition; for a Turk, on sea or land, never moves abroad unarmed. Her stores were in charge of a good steward, and a Nubian slave was attached to her as cook.

Acting as master of such a barge as this, the reader will not for a moment doubt that Alick had long cherished the idea of an escape, eventually, to his native land; and had it not been that he would have left his heart behind him, with the lovely daughter of the sultan, the fair Princess Esmah, he would, at all hazards, have attempted to escape long since. The unbounded confidence placed in him by the sultan, caused him to be no less respected than the highest officers of state, and he could come and go unchallenged. Thus, with a flowing sail and flaunting flags, he often dashed down the Bosphorus into the waters of the Black Sea, accompanied only by the slaves that formed the crew of the lugger, and these, too, almost all of his own countrymen, whose natural quickness and aptness of character peculiarly fitted them for seamen; besides which, doubtless Alick had his own object in selecting Greeks for his crew; he might some day turn their national spirit to account in escaping.

Esmah was well aware of the ease with which the page might leave her, and seek his native land; and the fact of his remaining true to her, under such circumstances, proved to her more indelibly the strength and sincerity of his love. They had even discussed earnestly the possibility of an escape together; but this was next to impossible, since the harem was so closely guarded at all hours; and then there was hardly the shadow of a chance for her, encountering so much publicity, even disguised, as she would have to do, in order to get on board the lugger without her father, and yet not be discovered. But the page could contemplate the idea of an escape from his present captivity only with Esmah as his companion. He did not desire liberty without her—love made him a willing captive.

"Sweet is bondage beneath the light of thy dear eyes, Esmah," the page would say.

"Nay, Alick, you flatter so cunningly, that one believes every word you utter."

"Flattery is useless, Esmah, where truth serves so well," the page would reply.

"What! again? Why, thou art the prince of flatterers, Alick," replied Esmah, archly, "and producest thy ware as old Mustapha does his perfumes—double distilled."

"True love, Esmah, never descends to flattery, for the heart is too full of honest emotions to seek for foreign and insincere ones. Besides, in flattery there is open deceit, and that true

ove never descends to. Nay, Esmah, I never uttered one
hought to thee, one single sentiment, that was not honest."

" I do believe thee, Alick, and did but jest when I spoke of
lattery."

" You recall the word, then, Esmah?" said the page, smiling.

" I do, and will offend no more, believe me," she replied.

" Say what thou wilt, I will never chide thee, dear Esmah."

" Not if I call thee flatterer?" said Esmah, archly.

" Nay, even then thou art forgiven before the offence is
committed."

With such charms of mind and tenderness of heart as we have
already referred to, Esmah possessed a person that would have
fired the imagination of a far less susceptible mind than that of
the page. Her figure, though slight, was yet beautifully rounded in the mould that was peculiar to her descent. The fine
native color of her lips and cheeks needed no foreign aid to
heighten them, and her soft, fair complexion seemed a miracle
in a land of swarthy skins. But, above all, her eyes were most
beautiful, even among such fine orbs as one is sure to meet with
in the Turks, for who ever saw a common or inexpressive eye
in the East? Those of the Princess Esmah were large, languid, and dreamy, shaded by the darkest and longest of lashes,
and beaming forth upon you the whole unrestrained soul of the
owner; eyes such as the vales of Circassia can alone account
for. Add to all, the poetical grace and perfection of figure that
crowned her youthful beauty, and the reader will not be surprised at the ardent and romantic devotion of the young Greek,
or even that he preferred slavery with her to freedom alone.

The peculiar situation of the page did not debar him from
much enjoyment, and from being exercised with a feeling of
pride in the fine craft of which he was the master, and which
he had been permitted to improve and beautify after his own
skill and taste, until she was really an object of admiration to
all nautical men who visited the port.

It is a gay summer afternoon, and the harbor of Constantinople, with all its gaudy and picturesque surroundings, is filled
with shipping. Now the sturdy " Ship-a-hoy!" of some English
seaman booms over the water, and now the shrill cry of the
Eastern mariners, and the liquid Turkish order, given from the
quarter-deck to the boy aloft. Yonder lie the heavy ships of
the Ottoman fleet, in moody silence. Here shoots by a graceful
caique, with its long, sharp prow and glittering ornaments,

filled with bearded and turbaned Turks; another follows close, filled with women wearing the *yashmac*, or veil of white muslin, covering all the face save the eyes and nose. Here are Armenian merchants returning from the city to their dwellings at Pera,—none but the faithful may sleep in the city of the prophet —dressed each in a costume which might set up an English merchant in business, from its wealth of jewels.

And now comes gliding up from the Black Sea, with its two lofty white sails, and the sacred color of the sultan flying at the peak, the Golden Horn. The master stands with the tiller in his hand; it is Alick, the Greek slave. Dropping his sails he rounds to, under the force of the current which sets into the Bosphorus from the north, and drops his anchor just under the Seraglio Point, in its deep, clear waters—a sacred spot, where none intrude.

An observant person might have noticed that whenever the Golden Horn sailed without some officers of the sultan's household on board, her prow was invariably turned towards the less inviting course of the Black Sea, rather than that of Marmora, notwithstanding this required her to struggle with the current that ever set towards the Ægean Sea and the waters of the Mediterranean. The fact was, that this northern course only took Alick, at every tack, further from his native land, and when the sultan first gave his slave the permission which he still enjoyed, it was to sail to the north!

Even now, though the Greek was so devoted to his service, and although he shared so much of his royal master's confidence, it may be justly doubted whether the sultan would have wished to trust his page alone in the direction of the Dardanelles with so fleet a craft as the Golden Horn beneath his fleet, and a four-knot current constantly setting down upon the isles of the Archipelago and the shores of Negropont and Greece itself!

"Our captain never sails to the south," said the mate of the lugger to his superior one day, rather in a tone of interrogatory than that of surprise.

The page looked at him, and marked well the expression of intelligence that the speaker wore upon his face. He was a Greek, like himself, and might be trusted.

"The course is open, and the wind free, on the Black Sea, and there's plenty of room there."

"True, captain, but the *current* sets through the waters of

Marmora and to the south," replied the mate, significantly, trying to read the expression of the page's eyes.

" It does," said the page, thoughtfully, "and we may try its force one of these days, brother."

" When?" asked the mate, eagerly, laying his hand upon his superior's arm.

" In time—in time," said the page.

"Stay," said his mate, seriously, while he looked about them to see that he was not overheard.

" Well, what would you?" asked his captain.

"A clipped bird longs for its wings again," said the mate, metaphorically, for he hardly dared speak plainer, even to Alick.

" I understand thee; we may fly that way anon," answered the Greek.

" The sooner the better," replied the mate, in a whisper, as the page turned away.

It was true that Alick had never laid his course to the southward further than the mouth of the Bosphorus, except with his royal master or some of the court on board the lugger. Yet he did not doubt that he might do so, perhaps, and not be reprimanded by the sultan, or challenged by the forts that frown so ominously at the mouth of the Dardanelles, like two austere sentinels at their posts. But for the sake of greater security and caution, the Greek shrewdly determined not to make the attempt until he had resolved in his own mind to escape from the sultan's service, and thus he would prevent any suspicion of his intended object.

When sailing in the waters referred to, the Greek had minutely studied the course of the varying channel, and marked, with an observant eye, where he could gain a point, and where avoid the shot of the two forts, should he happen ever to find himself in a situation to dread them; and it was doubtful if there was a pilot in all the sultan's service that knew the bottom of those waters so well as did the page.

CHAPTER V.

THE MEETING IN THE SERAGLIO GARDENS.

THE varying thread of our story now takes us to the far-famed perfume bazaar of Constantinople. Stay! what a cloud of perfume and sweet scents burthens the air! Here are gathered all the sweets of the far east and the west, from the long flacon of cologne to the tiny, gilded bottles of attar-gul, the aroma of burnt spices, delicate mixtures of rose and musk, with burning pestles of rarest flavor and most costly ingredients, calling to mind the sweets of "Araby the blest."

Bartering for some trifling article of perfume at the bazaar, stood a young Greek, in the national dress of his people, with a short Spanish cloak of blue broadcloth thrown slightly about his shoulders, as if to protect the wearer from the night dew, which already began to fall. He seemed to be less engaged, after all, with the scent-merchant than in anxiously looking about him in the expectation of meeting some other person. Anon, a female, clothed in the ample dress of white which causes all the sex to look alike in the streets of Constantinople, and her features so hidden as to puzzle all conjecture as to whom she might be, approached, and, purchasing a small flask of otto of rose, exchanged a hurried and secret greeting with the Greek, and both turned together from the perfume bazaar.

It was Alick and Esmah, who frequently made this a place of rendezvous when the regular meetings, as already described, in the presence of the father of the latter were interrupted. Sometimes, many days would transpire when they could only meet in this way, their appointments being made by sending some token, one to the other, by the dwarf.

"Can you meet me to-night within the seraglio gardens, Esmah?" he asked.

"At the bent cypress, Alick?" inquired the princess.

" Yes, dearest."

"I will try to do so, Alick," said Esmah, almost despondingly.

"Try, Esmah?"

"Yes; but I am watched most closely of late, Alick, and I think my mother suspects something of our intimacy. I tremble to think of it even for a moment; it would cost you your life if we were detected alone together, and at night."

"But to-night, dearest, we must meet. I have that to propose which will require secrecy and time to communicate, and, for better security, I will be there dressed as you are now; and it will puzzle old Brumah to detect me, I think."

"Heaven protect you, Alick!" replied the devoted girl, turning away.

"Good-by, dearest, until ten; at the bent cypress, by the fountains," said the Greek.

"Stay," said Esmah; "if I do not come, I will send you a line of the reason by the dwarf. So now good-night—we may be discovered here."

"Good-night," repeated the page, watching her loved form until it turned an angle of the Mosque of St. Sophia, the mosque of mosques, the St. Peter's of Constantinople.

The performance of some duty prescribed by his royal master, drew the page across the Bosphorus to the pretty village of Arnaoult-Keni, where a spectacle met his eyes which seemed to be almost prophetic as it regarded his own situation at that very time. The bodies of a Turkish woman and a young Greek hung from the shutters of a window on the water's side. Alick learned, by inquiry, that the Greek had been detected in leaving her house at daybreak, and, in less than an hour after, the lovers were hanging side by side in death!

Reflecting upon this summary mode of execution, and knowing that the poor victims were often taken before the petty judge and condemned on mere suspicion, and then hurried to execution, the page reviewed his own situation with a sense of uneasiness that he had never before experienced; but he cheered himself with the idea that he should soon be removed from so precarious a situation, and took his boat back again to the seraglio. The passage carried him directly over the spot where, as a boy from the Trebizond slave-ship, he had saved the child, whom he afterwards so dearly loved, from a tragical end. His thoughts reverted to the scene, and recalled a whole volume of his life, from that period to the present. In this mood he landed, and passed within the palace gates.

That night, as the full, clear moon came up from behind the hills of Stamboul, and tipped the golden minarets of the seraglio gardens, Alick and Esmah sat together under the deep shadows of an ancient and low-bent cypress. They were not unobserved by the jealous eye of Brumah, chief of the eunuchs; but his vision was poor, and age had commenced to lay its thin veil upon his sight. So the household officer took both to be of the same sex, and respected their privacy, though once he seemed to suspect that all was not right, and had turned with evident design to approach and accost them; but scarcely had he advanced a dozen steps towards the two lovers, when a toy petard was fired by some unknown hand close behind him, startling his nerves by its unexpected explosion, and quite disconcerting his equanimity for some time, drawing him off to discover from whence it came, but this he found in vain. The page understood the trick at once, and knew full well that it was a device of the dwarf to prevent their being discovered. It was successful, for Brumah was driven completely away from the point, in his irritable search after the culprit who had played him this annoying trick.

The Greek told the princess that he could no longer live thus near to her, be able to see her but by stealth, or under such restraint as to preclude all interchange of feeling, and that he had at length resolved to fly from the service of her father immediately. He begged of her to attempt an escape with him, disguised in the dress of a page—pointed out to her the plan he had matured for this purpose—told her that he had already organized his crew for the voyage, and had stored the lugger with care and secrecy. This had been done by degrees, and the Golden Horn was at that moment prepared for a long cruise. He told her that if she would consent to fly with him, he would make her his honored wife by sacred marriage; and that they would, with the morning sun both be on board the yacht, and, with all things prepared, would boldly sail away from the Seraglio Point, and seek a home in his native land. He drew a golden picture, in his enthusiasm and love, but Esmah looked thoughtful and almost sad while the page thus spoke.

"Alick, you know that I dearly love my father—that it is hard, very hard, to leave him thus. But I am thine, wholly thine; do with me as thou wilt!" said the devoted and confiding girl, her soft hand within his own, and her soul beaming from her eyes.

Esmah did not name her mother, for though she respected her relationship, yet her parent was a person so vastly different from her daughter, so childish, fond only of jewelry, and paying no attention to Esmah, save a sort of jealous watchfulness, that the princess could hardly love and respect her mother as she would have done one with whom she could have associated with some feelings in common. Her mother was still the beautiful, still the favorite wife of her proud consort, the sultan; but there her attractions ended.

"Can you forego all the comforts of your palace home, to wander with me, Esmah?" asked the Greek, thoughtfully.

"Your presence would make any home a palace for Esmah," replied the gentle girl, drawing still nearer to his side as she thus spoke the warm promptings of her heart.

"When I betray such confidence and love as thine, may Heaven forsake me!" said the Greek, earnestly, as he fondly pressed the little hand he held.

Though Brumah had thus been diverted from his customary vigilance, still he had again resumed his rounds, and was near to the broken cypress, when Alick thought it time for them to separate, and he whispered to Esmah:

"You understand the plan in full—the place and the hour?"

"At sunrise, on the shore, in the dress that you gave me," replied Esmah.

"Punctually, Esmah, for a few moments' delay might betray all."

"I will be there on the moment."

"For to-night, then, farewell," said the page, stealing a kiss from the fair hand he had been clasping.

"Farewell," whispered Esmah, with a quick-beating heart, hurrying away to the sacred and prison-like apartments of the sultan's harem, where she might prepare herself for the exciting programme laid out for the morrow.

The page sought his own apartment in the palace, not without the exercise of some caution, however, to avoid the prying eyes of Brumah, who seemed to be imbued with a spirit of jealousy concerning every one, and, after preparing a few trifles for the morrow, he sat down and tried to compose his mind for thought. But he was restless and anxious; to-morrow was to decide his fate and that of Esmah, and how could he be composed? Now he walked the rich, soft carpet of his room with a hurried and nervous step, and now he threw himself upon the clustered

3

cushions that were piled luxuriantly against the wall.   At last
he seized his guitar, and, in a low, musical voice, sang a song
of his boyhood and his native land:

"My own bright Greece! my sunny land!
    Nurse of the brave and free!
How bound the cords beneath my hand
    Whene'er I think of thee!
The myrtle branches wave above my brow
And glorious memories throng around me now."

At last, wearied and almost exhausted with mental and physical excitement, he fell asleep, to dream of the plans he had
formed for the morrow, and to enjoy visions of happiness and
love.

The earliest gray of the morning saw the page upon the
quarter-deck of the lugger.   Everything was quiet about her,
no suspicious hurry was evinced; and a young Greek boy who
was washing down the forward deck, seemed to do it as leisurely
as though 'the whole day was before him for his task.   Yet a
seaman would have observed that the lugger was ready to sail
at a moment's notice.   Her anchors were stowed, her fore and
main sails were loose and ready for hoisting, while she rode by
a single stern-fast from her quarter to the shore.   Every rope
was neatly coiled away, and there was nothing loose upon her
decks; even the guns were carefully secured.   A broad plank
lay from the bulwarks to the shore, so close could the yacht lay
to the landing.   One single order would have cleared everything
in a moment, and left the lugger free to slip away upon the current to the southward; and Alick had joyfully noted that the
wind was off the Asian shore, and most favorable for his
enterprise.

The Greek was looking first anxiously towards the eastern
horizon, and to the portal whence he expected to see Esmah
appear, dressed as a page.   At last, as the color deepened in
the east, and the sun's rich light heralded its coming, Alick
grew so impatient as to be hardly able to contain himself, until
at last the broad face of the king of day itself burst forth above
the horizon!

At that moment, a large hound which belonged to the page,
but which was the pet and companion of Esmah, came leaping
with the speed of the wind towards the lugger, and, seeing its
well-beloved master on the deck, with one immense bound it

leaped from the shore to his side, and, fawning affectionately upon him, endeavored to attract his notice. But the page was too anxious to notice even this favorite animal, thinking that possibly Esmah might have sent him before to herald her coming. He still gazed towards the seraglio gates. But still the hound seemed to fawn upon his master with uncommon earnestness, until the boy forward, coming aft, said:

"There's a bit of paper tied to the dog's neck, sir. Perhaps you didn't see?"

"I did not, indeed," replied Alick, hastily tearing a billet from the hound's collar; and opening it, the following lines met his startled vision:

"We are discovered! Fly at once,—if not for your own sake, for mine! There is not one moment to lose—the officers are already aroused. The dwarf will send you this on the hound's neck. Farewell! Heaven protect thee, Alick, and grant that we may meet again under happier auspices! Esmah."

"Gracious heaven! how this business has miscarried!" he exclaimed, crushing the note.

The page saw in a moment that, in her endeavors to keep her appointment, the princess had been discovered, and probably this, coupled with former suspicions on her mother's part, had led to an expose. He trembled for her safety, for he knew that the customs of the people were so rigid that a suspected person was rarely permitted to live; and he thought that the sultan, devoted as he was to Esmah, might be persuaded by others to form the severest opinion of his child, and perhaps even to execute the ordinary law upon her, which would consign her to death by the sack in the waters of the Bosphorus. But Alick feared to stay. He knew he could do her no good, and possibly that he might prejudice her situation still more by remaining, and so resolved to follow her direction as contained in the note.

A low but shrill whistle upon a silver call at his neck brought a half score of ready hands upon deck in an instant. A silent order severed the stern-fast, and another set the fore and main sail of the lugger, and with Alick at the helm, the Golden Horn shot away from the Seraglio Point like an arrow from a bow!

The die was cast—he had taken an irretrievable step, one that he could not retrace; that step made the sultan and the laws of Turkey his enemy. His brain was crowded for the instant with contending emotions—regret at leaving Esmah, a

half-undefined joy at a thrilling sense of liberty as he boldly
turned the lugger's head to the south, and a partial realization
of the risk he was encountering, all came up at a single thought.
He bit his lips with vexation at the failure of his plot for Esmah's
escape with him, but what availed it now to regret? The Ru-
bicon was passed. And he turned his thoughts to the care of
the yacht. Her sheets were loosened, and the sultan's colors
hoisted at the peak, for Alick knew full well that he had four
fortifications to pass, the guns of either of which might sink him
at one discharge; but by boldly displaying the sacred colors, he
trusted that he might be able to pass them all before the alarm
could be given or suspicion aroused. If he should be followed,
he had such confidence in the speed of the Golden Horn, that
he could outsail all pursuit.

As he fairly laid his course to the southward, and the lugger
felt the force of the current, as well as that of her sails, impel-
ling her swiftly into the Sea of Marmora, the young Greek heard
the steady roll of the drum, and the regular beat to arms, that
he knew full well had followed an order for his immediate
arrest by the soldiery.

CHAPTER VI.

A SEA CHASE IN DETAIL.

WE left the page, in the last chapter, gliding swiftly down the
Sea of Marmora with the Golden Horn, in his escape from the
Sultan Mahomet's service after the discovery of the plot he had
formed for carrying off the Princess Esmah. Alick forgot that
from the moment he cut the stern-fast that secured the lugger to
the Seraglio Point, he became a *pirate*, for such even now is the
law of nations. He might have escaped personally, without,
perhaps, much danger of detection, at least with ordinary pre-
caution. But in taking the sultan's yacht he was making a bold
move and running a vast deal of additional risk.

He could touch at no port even in Greece, where he could be
secure from seizure, nor could he land in safety at any spot,
from Malta up the sea to Gibraltar. All this he began to realize
as he cleared the Dardanelles and opened the Ægean Sea.
However, his heart was comparatively light, for he was once

more free; and he only thought with regret of Esmah. His active imagination pictured her in every conceivable dilemma, and all on account of her intimacy with him, and her love for her father's slave. He felt now how dear she was to him, now that every moment served to divide them further from each other. He began to forget his own situation in his anxiety about her he loved. The fearful picture that he had witnessed at Arnaoult-Keni, of the two lovers executed together, was still before his eyes, and he even feared that the vengeance of the sultan and his people might be reeked upon her whom he had left behind. He reasoned against this by adducing the fact of her father's deep regard and love for his child. But still he knew Turkish justice, as it is called, to be most fearfully headstrong, and that her father in his vengeance might believe Esmah already guilty, and condemn her to death. In this frame of mind Alick became moody and thoughtful, so much so as to attract the notice of his crew, who wondered that he could feel thus at such a moment, and one or two even asked the mate what could so depress their young commander.

"He is often thus," replied the mate, evasively.

But at the same time he resolved to probe his captain, and satisfy his own curiosity; and for this purpose he engaged in some ordinary piece of a seaman's duty that should bring him upon the quarter-deck of the lugger.

"You are gloomy, captain," said the second in command, respectfully saluting the page. "Surely this is no time for regrets, when we are getting on so well."

"True, true," said the page, hurriedly: "as you say, this is no time for grief, for we have been thus far very successful."

This remark was followed by an order or two from the page, in relation to the sailing gear of the lugger, and then he relapsed into his thoughtful mood again, secretly regretting that he had ever proposed an enterprise that could possibly separate him from Esmah, and actually wishing himself back again once more by her side in quiet, and unsuspected of treachery to his late master the sultan.

"Perhaps you are sick?" suggested the mate, whose business again brought him near to his commander's side, and who wondered at the moody spirit of Alick.

"O, no, not at all, my good friend. I was thinking of the romantic legends that attach themselves to these headlands hereaway. This is a most interesting spot, crowded with legend and story," replied the page, struggling to regain his wonted cheerfulness.

"I don't see much of interest here," said the mate, listlessly.

"You have sailed in these waters before?" asked the page.

"O, yes, from a boy, until captured and carried to Constantinople."

"And never heard of the past history of these points?"

"Not particularly. There was a big English ship cast away just off Fures within my memory."

"I mean the legends of the years gone by, of olden times, when mighty deeds marked the passage."

"Well, now the sinking of a big ship is something to remember," said the mate.

"Yes, as a fearful accident, to be sure," replied his captain; "but I am talking of the records of history—facts that occurred long before our time, or that of our fathers."

"Yes. That's a good way back, though, captain."

"See you naught of interest here?" said the page, rather thinking aloud than addressing his assistant.

"I have heard a good deal said about the Dardanelles and the Upper Ægean, but I don't see anything very remarkable here," said the mate, glancing first at the European and then at the Asiatic shore of the pass. "I have had my eyes on those two forts, there, that flank the near approach of the two continents,. but we are out of reach of them now," continued the mate, with evident satisfaction.

The page heeded not the remark of his less romantic and intelligent companion, but as if aroused to a different train of thought by his own reference to the history of the scene about them, he looked thoughtfully around.

"Here was drowned Helle, daughter of Athamas, king of Thebes," said the page, still musing to himself.

The mate looked in all directions with staring eyes, as though he expected to see the ghost of the dead princess arise from the sea.

"And here, too, the gallant Leander perished," continued the page, thoughtfully.

As to Leander, the mate seemed to be puzzled, but shrewdly thought he might have been captain of some fishing-smack of the Archipelago.

"And here, between Sestos and Abydos, Xerxes's ill-fated host crossed in their bridge of boats," still mused the page, half leaning upon the bulwarks as he looked off towards the points he referred to.

This reference to the history of the past completed the mystification of the mate, who, in his bewilderment, began to scan the distance, rather than the view nearest to them, when suddenly he seemed to discover something that was calculated to arouse both him and his master from their musings on the past, to a most vivid realization of the present and its vicissitudes.

"Look hither, captain," said the mate. "See you not, just off the castle of Moito, a sail that looks much like one of the sultan's ships we left anchored off the Seraglio Point, when we slipped our cable this morning?"

The page started from his thoughtful attitude at these words, and seizing a glass, looked intently in the direction indicated by his second in command. The lugger had already swept with a fine breeze that came tripping off the shores of Asia far to the south, and some three leagues already lay between her and the fortress referred to. Trusting to the fleet character of the yacht, the page had scarce a doubt that he should be able to escape without trouble; but the sail now referred to, seemed to indicate that the most prompt exertions had been adopted to overtake him. Besides, a glance told him that the frigate had made far better time than the lugger, for she must have lost at least an hour in getting under weigh after the alarm was given.

"By this light, it is the Mahomet—the fastest frigate in the sultan's fleet!" said the page, still examining her through the glass.

"'Tis the Mahomet, indeed," said the mate, despondingly.

"Starboard your helm a bit," said the page, "and bring her head more to the south."

"Starboard," repeated the man at the helm, as he obeyed the order.

The bows of the lugger fell off a couple of points, taking the full force of the land breeze right aft, and jibing his foresail, the page skimmed along in the favorite style of a fore-and-aft rig. But still the Golden Horn, even in this her best point of sailing, did not seem to distance her pursuer so fast as to make any gain apparent to the now anxious eye of the page. The fact was, Alick had put the lugger on this point to test the fact to his own satisfaction, for he knew very well that he could not long stand upon that course, and that he must soon tack, to weather the Isle of Shoals.

This was soon the case, for the mate, who had been sent forward in the lookout at the bows, declared the water to be shoaling fast, which was met with a prompt order from the page to go about. This manœuvre brought the lugger's head to the southward and eastward, and the wind having also hauled a little to the northward, enabled her to lay a more southerly course, close-hauled, and to speed merrily on towards the Isles of the Archipelago, where Alick felt that he could take advantage of his old knowledge of the varying channels and reefs, to puzzle the commander of the sultan's ship, who would not dare to follow him into such shoal water and so precarious navigation.

In the meantime the mate had been rigging up a sort of jigger-sail aft, the spar being stepped just by the tafferel, as a sort of additional impetus to the lugger—a sail much used in those days, and more latterly in these inland seas, to crowd the bows of the craft well up to the wind, enabling them to steer small, as sailors say, close in the wind's eye. But the new sail was a mere speck compared with the broad and lofty sheets that the frigate was every moment adding to her studding-sail booms, which had not until now been set.

The mate desisted from his job of rigging out a jigger, and at a suggestion from Alick, even took it in, as it could do them no good. The lugger was making all the speed she could, before a fair wind, but the wind was as favorable for the ship as it was for the lugger, and while the latter had been tacking, the ship had laid her course steadily for the south, hoping, evidently, to head the lugger off from the islands and the open sea beyond. By means of her loftier sails, she was now gaining perceptibly upon the yacht, so that by nightfall, as the land breeze died away, and a dead calm set in, the two vessels were little less than two leagues from each other, and almost motionless.

"I would have staked my all on the speed of the lugger," said the mate to Alick; "but she has seemed to drag along like a sick cur to-day."

"You mistake," replied the page. "Consider first your impatience, and the extraordinary speed of the Mahomet, and you will see she has done well."

The mate saw the force of the remark, but looked disappointed, nevertheless.

"He has overhauled us hand over hand ever since we first made him out at the Dardanelles," continued the mate.

"True," replied the page, "but his spread of canvas aloft is immense."

"Only enough to make up the increased depth of water that she draws," continued the mate, sadly dissatisfied with their luck, and inclined to lay all blame upon the lugger, which Alick, true seaman-like, was anxious to defend.

"Remember that a deep craft *with* the current is all the better," said the page. "We who set so lightly upon it feel but half its power."

Alick was too much of a philosopher and too good a seaman for his mate to argue with, had not discipline forbade such familiarity—for although they were in common there, all Greeks, endeavoring to escape from a barbarous slavery, still all looked up to the page with respect and duty, for his very nature was such as to command these tokens from those about him.

"Get out a couple of sweeps forward," said the page, "and we will keep her in motion."

The night was remarkably clear, and even at the distance which intervened between the two vessels, the crew of either could see the others busy at the sweeps; in addition to which, the frigate had a half dozen boats out ahead towing, but if any change was perceptible in the relative positions of the two, it was in favor of the lugger, as her light draft of water rendered her more manageable in calm weather, and more obedient to the sweeps.

It was an anxious night on board the yacht. Not an eye was closed, not a hand unemployed, and every one worked as though life depended upon the issue. But the longest night must have an end, and as day broke, a slight breeze sprang up with the sun, and both the frigate and the lugger felt its enlivening power at the same instant, and at once began to move through the water with lifelike spirit and motion.

The lugger was manned by about a score of Greeks, besides Alick and his mate, but the idea of resistance seemed almost preposterous under the existing circumstances, as a single broadside from the frigate, if fairly aimed and within gunshot, would inevitably blow the lugger out of water. Still Alick knew that the guns he carried were of a remarkable bore, and designed for the long shot, and as the frigate came up now hand over hand, he felt that his vessel bore a sort of charmed life, since no shot from the frigate had touched her.

It seemed for awhile as though the lugger herself rejoiced at

the lucky shots that had been fired from her decks, for she seemed to have gathered renewed powers, and was shooting like a bird on the wing down the southern current that makes towards the Grecian Archipelago. But the frigate's people, as if all patience were lost by the effect of the shots from the lugger, yawned gracefully to for a moment and fired a dozen well-aimed shots towards the Golden Horn, at a single discharge.

"Luff—luff quick, I say!" shouted the page, as he saw the movement of the frigate; for as he was stern on, her broadside must have raked him fore and aft had the lugger not minded her helm and rounded up, gracefully fore-reaching twice her own length.

"That touch at her fore rigging hit in a tender spot," said Alick to the mate, who was on the quarter-deck tending the guns.

"Yes, and so he's sending us his compliments—there they come, ripping up the sea, and tossing the water like mad."

"Half of those will go astern of us, thanks to the manner in which the lugger fore-reaches," said Alick, marking well the course of the shot as they came.

All eyes were now watching the dread messengers.

"Down, for your lives, every one of you—flat, I say, upon the deck!" shouted the page, with an energy of tone that thrilled the crew.

In the meantime the yacht was shaking in the wind, and yet forging slightly ahead from the impetus of her headway when the helm was put down, and these incidents, that have taken so much space to describe, had transpired in about two minutes of time.

"Steady, there!" said Alick, as a last word of warning to his crew.

The shot came dancing as merrily over the waves as though their mission was not a bloody one. But alas! a fearful crash was heard on board the yacht, as the splinters flew from her side, and the groans of two wounded men followed the discharge from the frigate.

As soon as the iron messengers had done their mission, the bows of the lugger were once more brought to the south. This was not done, however, without some considerable trouble, as the current had now got the craft broadside on, and was sweeping it thus with its courses. There being no longer any headway on the lugger, of course she could not mind her helm.   A

few moments' labor at one of the sweeps on the weather bow soon brought her round, and as soon as she took the wind in her foresail, all was right again, and she was once more thoroughly in hand.

The commander of the Mahomet, in his eagerness to deliver his broadside into the lugger, came near getting into the same difficulty, and came round to his course again most lazily, though he was enabled to do so with his topsails—an advantage that a square-rig has over a plain fore-and-after. The confusion caused on board the frigate by the wounded spars and sails referred to, was very manifest on board the lugger, and Alick remarked:

" Another such mishap, my friend Hafiz, and you will have to lay by and repair damages."

" Fire high," continued Alick, to one of the men by his side, who was now pointing one of the pieces; " it's his rigging we want to harm."

The man obeyed, and taking the hint, fired another shot among the fore-sheets that sent a couple of ropes upon the deck by the run, and dropped the top-gallant-sail upon the cap beneath.

" Well done," said Alick; " keep up that play, my man."

Again the captain of the frigate brought his broadside to bear upon the lugger, and again Alick performed the same manoeuvre as before, taking care this time not to lose command of the lugger so far as before, and after receiving the shot without further damage, he turned again to the south.

The mate went forward at a sign from his young commander, to help the wounded, while Alick ground his teeth in silence, and all the fire of his native spirit seemed roused by the blood he saw spilled from his fellow-countrymen. A cool determination of spirit seemed to be overspreading his countenance, and he became calmer than he had seemed at any previous moment during the chase.

The wounded men were conveyed below. Not a word was spoken on board the lugger. The page had himself taken the helm, and still the beautiful yacht sped on like a wounded deer, as fleet as ever, no vital spot being touched, and she seemed to be only spurred forward by the shot that had struck her hull and rigging. The calm determination of purpose evinced in the page's face had also communicated itself to his crew, and they stood there unmoved and resolved.

CHAPTER VII.

DESTRUCTION OF THE LUGGER.

IT is proverbial that the Turks are bad sailors, but the captain of the Mahomet happened to be an exception to the general rule, and he was now out-manœuvering the lugger, notwithstanding the loss of some of his head sails, and was fast closing with her. As the crisis approached, the native fire in the bosom of the page burned clearer and brighter. He summoned his men aft, and asked them if they would stand to their arms, and fight to the last, to which they all enthusiastically responded in the affirmative—for they had no wish to return to Constantinople to die by the bowstring, or be strangled in the open streets, as an example to their former companions in slavery. Realizing that this would be their inevitable fate if they were taken by the frigate, the Greeks declared that they would rather sink with the lugger than fall again into the hands of the Turks.

The page had now duly considered their situation, and he fully comprehended its danger. He did not feel authorized to risk the lives of the crew further, unless by their own free consent. For himself, he would gladly fight to the last, and die with his sword in his hand. He summoned them aft, pointed out to them that their lives were at stake,—that if taken by the frigate, some of them, perhaps, might be pardoned, but the majority would doubtless be made examples of in Constantinople. He told them that he would be governed by their own wishes as to yielding up the lugger. But one voice came from those dauntless men. They declared that they would fight to the last, and that death itself was preferable to a return to their former state of slavery.

"It is well," said the page, after hearing their decision; "to your duty, then."

A hearty cheer rung from the little band as they went once more to their stations, although the light of hope must have beamed very dimly in their hearts.

The small arms of the lugger's armament had already been dealt out to the men, and the guns on the quarter-deck were kept hot by constant use. But splinters were flying from the sides of the Golden Horn as the frigate drew nearer, and three or four Greeks now lay severely wounded upon the deck forward; they only cheered on their companions, however, and some good marksmen among them were picking off the crew and officers of the frigate as she neared them; and the excitement on board the Mahomet told how fatal the Greeks were in their aim. Indeed, as it afterwards appeared, the three lieutenants of the frigate were thus killed. At this moment, a lucky shot from the lugger, striking near where a former one had hit, brought down the fore-topmast of the frigate from the cap, and greatly impeded the way, by the wreck that dragged alongside, as well as entangling the rest of the fore sheets.

"Hurra!" shouted the excited Greeks from their little craft.

"This is encouraging," said the page to his mate; "haul the sheets well aft, and trim her close down to it. The frigate must fall off a little now."

"Minutes are hours to us now," replied the mate, obeying the order.

The wounding of the Mahomet's foremast enabled the lugger to shoot ahead once more, almost out of gunshot from the frigate, before the latter could sufficiently repair the damage to resume her wonted speed. But the captain of the sultan's frigate was now exasperated; and though he had refrained from pouring his entire broadside into the lugger, from a hope of retaking her without much injury to her hull and spars, he now resolved to pour all his fire upon the devoted yacht. For this purpose his guns were double-shotted, and orders were given to fire *low* at the hull and decks of the Golden Horn.

The northern headlands of Negropont had already hove in sight, and Alick and his remaining companions were spurred on to renewed exertion by the sight of their native land, towards which they were gradually approaching. The Golden Horn, now sadly wounded and torn by the shots, with more than one large leak from those that had struck her about the water-line, and her deck stained with blood, still held on towards the rocky and dangerous shore of Negropont, and this, too, although the prudent captain of the frigate had shortened sail, for he knew the dangerous character of the navigation, and he had already run in as near as he dared to do with his draft of water. But the lugger could hold on safely much longer.

"How is the water forward?" asked the page of his mate at this critical moment.

"We are shoaling it fast, and the lugger settles every moment," was the reply.

"How many of the men are alive yet, forward there?" asked the page.

"Seven," was the reply.

"Shoal water is our only hope," said the page. "Heaven send that we find enough to carry us to the shore without touching!"

"We are settling every moment," said the mate, measuring the draft of water.

Alick still hoped to reach the shore before the lugger should sink, but the leaks were gaining fast upon them, and she could hold on but a short time longer. Now and then a shot would strike her from the frigate, and the splinters would fly like a shower of hailstones about his head, while his comrades lay dead and dying about him. His own guns had been silenced for some time, but he held the tiller with a firm hand, and looked sternly towards the rock-bound coast before him. Hope was still in his heart, and stern resolve beamed forth from his eye.

"Farewell, brother!" said the mate to Alick, waving his hand to him from under one of the guns, which he had managed so well during the action, and where a spent ball had now laid him fatally wounded.

"Farewell, my brave comrade. God speed you to paradise!" replied the page, leaning over and pressing the hand of the dying man.

"Greece and liberty!" shouted the mate, faintly, and fell back a lifeless corpse.

Scarce half a dozen of the Greeks were left alive, and all these were more or less wounded. But, with earnest eyes bent on their young commander, they remained silent, and unmoved by any outward token, awaiting his order or their fate.

It was already night once more, so stubborn and so close had been the chase. Flitting clouds swam swiftly in the aerial sea, the young moon was now hidden for a moment, and all was darkness as if a frown came from the sky upon the fearful scene below; the next instant the frigate's people saw the lugger sud-

denly stop short, tremble, and fall to pieces, while the waves
seemed to engulf her hull and spars as if by magic. Her bows
had struck a sunken rock, some half league from the shore,
and her already weakened frame proved too frail to survive the
shock. No sign of life remained of the lugger or her people.
All, all were gone!

> "O, was the spoiler's vessel nigh?
> Yes! there becalmed in silent sleep,
> Dark and alone on a breathless deep,
> On a sea of molten silver, dark,
> Brooding, it frowned—that evil bark!"
>
> HEMANS.

Humanity is no part of a Turk's composition, at least so far
as it regards his converse with his fellow-man, more particularly
if he happens to be a Christian, though to the animal kingdom
his strict adherence to the principles and directions contained
in the Koran leads him to show the tenderest solicitude. And
thus the captain of the Mahomet did not so much as lower a
boat to see if any of the drowning men might not be saved.
Not he! it would have been more natural for him to listen to
their cries for help with gratification. The frigate lay by the
spot until the morning, and then, seeing no signs of any of the
lugger's crew, nor so much as a single spar left of the ill-fated
yacht, she squared away her sails and deliberately laid her
course to the north through the Dardanelles.

In due time the frigate arrived safely at her moorings in the
Bosphorus, and after her sails were furled, and everything done
in the slow, tedious etiquette of the Turkish style, the captain's
report was made in person to the sultan.

"Say you he fought so resolutely?" asked the sultan, musing.

"Highness, he fought like one resolved to sell his life dearly."

"And your loss in killed was how many?" asked the sultan.

"Three good officers, highness, and a score of able seamen."

"He had the guns on the quarter-deck, you say?" continued
the sultan, musing; for he, too, felt a pride in the lugger, and
all that was attached to her.

"Yes, highness,—pointing them with his own hands," replied
the captain of the Mahomet.

"And had nearly reached the coast of Greece?" continued
the sultan, much interested.

"The lugger sunk off the northern coast of Negropont,"
replied the officer.

"By the beard of the prophet, but we loved the boy," said the sultan, musing still.

"He knew the lugger, highness, and sailed her like an old seaman."

"There was true metal in Alick," replied the sultan.

"No seaman could deny that," said the master of the Mahomet.

The fate of the Greeks who had attempted to escape in the sultan's yacht, was published in all parts of the city, by the officers of the household, as an example to deter others from committing a like offence. But the sultan was sad, for he had really loved the boy who had been so long with him; indeed, he had grown to need the services of one who had studied to meet his every want, and even to anticipate them. The page had arranged his minutest matters for the sultan, who now felt like one lost without his valued services.

It was true that Esmah had been detected in the disguise that she had assumed to wear on board the lugger, and that her mother had raised the alarm that had led to the note which the princess sent to him. But the mother, fearing that the strict rules of the Turkish creed would be performed upon her child, managed shrewdly to hush the matter up, and make it appear that Esmah was in no way to blame; and indeed the sultan came to the conclusion that Alick only sought his own liberty and that of his comrades.

To prevent suspicion, Esmah was forced to a display of cheerfulness, that, although it belied her heart, yet dispelled all doubt as to her innocence. She was even gayer than usual, not from fear for herself, but lest the page's memory should suffer by any suspicion.

In private, however, the gentle girl gave full vent to the pent-up feelings of her heart. Alas! how bitterly did Esmah mourn! Her young heart seemed to be broken, for it was wholly given to the lost page. The first shock of the sad news was almost too much for her. First it caused her brain to reel, and her reason to vacillate; then it awoke a fierce and almost bloody fury in her heart, coupled with a cunning to accomplish her will that was entirely foreign to her nature. She walked the ample precincts of her own apartment in the harem with a flushed cheek, a quivering lip, and a bloodshot eye; she seemed no longer the gentle and lovely being that we have known her, but more like a tigress deprived of her young; all the evil of her nature was aroused and stimulated within her breast.

At last, in this strange and unnatural mood, she assumed a calmness that she was far from realizing, and sought her father. She began by adroitly representing his own loss in the absence of the page, pictured in fine colors the cruelty that had deprived a master of his slave, and showed the murderous conduct of the captain of the Mahomet in the most odious light, representing how far this officer had exceeded his authority, for, when sent to capture and bring back the page, he had not only caused his life to fall a sacrifice, but had also destroyed the yacht.

"Had he orders, father, to destroy yacht, page, Greeks, and all?"

"None, Esmah; he was sent but to recover our property," replied the sultan.

"But, in his better judgment and wisdom, he saw fit to destroy it?"

"Thus it seems," replied her father, who began to look at the matter in the light that Esmah desired, and to show some signs of dissatisfaction.

"One would think that a frigate so large as the Mahomet might have taken a pleasure-yacht without so much bloodshed, and the loss of so many lives and so much property on her own part," continued the princess, cunningly, adding fuel to the fire of her father's anger, which she saw was now momentarily increasing.

"True," said the sultan.

"It was *bravely* done, however, of yon captain of the frigate," added Esmah.

The sultan looked troubled, but did not reply to the remark.

"Do you not think it was well done by Captain Hafiz?" asked Esmah.

"By this light, it was not," replied the sultan, much ruffled.

Esmah saw that her task was done, and she turned and left him.

The sultan was sore on the loss of Alick; he was naturally impetuous, and his child's remarks had goaded him to a state of excitement and anger, and in the heat of his passion he sent for his chief executioner!

"Arissim!"

"Highness."

"Draw near to us."

4

" Your highness's slave," said the officer, making a profound salaam.

" You know the captain, Hafiz, of the Mahomet frigate?" asked the sultan.

" Highness, yes," replied the officer, bending in the Oriental style.

" He has displeased us."

" Highness, your enemies are only fit to feed the dogs," said the submissive official. " What are your commands?"

The sultan pointed significantly to his neck, and nodded to his executioner.

" Highness, I am your slave!" replied the man, again bending low before the sultan.

"Prepare me an order, and affix the seal," said the sultan.

The executioner, who was often and suddenly summoned, drew from the folds of his dress the desired articles, and, bending low, said:

" It is ready for your seal, highness."

This was at once affixed, and the official retired.

Arissim, supplied with the usual authority, turned his steps towards the frigate of which Captain Hafiz was the commander. The sultan's executioner is all-powerful in Turkey; his authority, once displayed, is never doubted, and his coming is a token that all understand. None dare to stay him, none to dispute his orders; he presents himself in silence before his victim, shows the insignia of the royal order, and commands the condemned one to follow him to the place that is appropriated for his punishment.

Thus Arissim summoned the commander of the frigate, who, glancing at the royal seal, bowed low in humble submission, and, without so much as pausing to express a wish or give an order to his people, with the true stoicism of the Turk, submitted to his fate without a murmur. To ask for an explanation, or to beg for time to explain, he knew would be utterly useless, and so followed the executioner at his will. In passing a mosque, he was permitted to enter for a moment to utter his brief prayer, and bend his body three times towards the tomb of the prophet, and then he followed on to his doom.

That very night the captain, Hafiz, of the frigate Mahomet, died by the bow-string. Such is Turkish justice!

CHAPTER VIII.

LIFE IN A TURKISH HAREM.

FIVE years have passed since the close of the last chapter—years of bustle and toil, of pleasure and of sorrow, in life's varied picture; but still the bright and luxuriant emporium of the East shines forth in all its Oriental splendor. Its bazaars still teem with prodigality in all matters of comfort, necessity and elegance. The caravans which move thither through the heart of Asia, still bring with them the rich silks and teas of China, the delicate muslins of Bengal, the gorgeous shawls of Cashmere, the costly gems of Golconda, and the pure gold and ivory of Africa; nor has modern nautical discovery and enterprise essentially affected this vast and restless tide of inland commerce.

And there rolls the far-famed Bosphorus still, with all the tragical interest of the past lingering about it, its blushing waters yet made the grave of suspected beauty, where remorseless jealousy has rudely buried so many charms. Here, of old, crossed the countless hosts of Persia in their fierce invasion of Europe; and over this stream, too, passed the Vandal and the Goth, to devastate, like a blight upon the land, the fairest portion of earth, and to lay waste the records and monuments of genius!

Could anything be more beautiful than the Bosphorus? with an extent of half a dozen leagues from Constantinople to the Black Sea, separating Asia and Europe by but half a mile of blue waters, and its shores lined the whole distance with villages, palaces, mosques, and minarets,—with little fairy-like houses, decked by endless ornaments, half hidden by the trees,—and the lofty, solemn cypresses that shade the beautiful cemeteries, held so sacred in the East,—with valleys stretching back from the shore into picturesque hills, the summits crowned with fairy-like kiosks, and a hundred other beauties that are so Oriental in their character. "See Naples and die," the Italians say; but a modern writer has substituted for Naples, Constantinople and the Bosphorus!

While all the rest of the busy world is steadily advancing in

intelligence and general civilization, the Turk is ever the same;
he changes not, but, associating his minutest actions with his
religion, he looks upon every deviation from the example of his
ancestors as a criminal departure from the spirit and principles of the Koran. Even experience fails to teach him improve-
ment, and, being too vain to be taught by others, he is also too
lazy to teach himself. Give him his pipe, coffee, and dish of
kibaub, and you may have all the rest of the world, provided
you do not cast too inquiring glances towards the doors of his
harem.

In his adherence to the dress of his nation, the Mussulman
shows a prominent trait of his character. It is not the classical
elegance and richness of the Cashmere that makes him love the
turban, but it is the fact that his ancestors wore it before him;
it is because they fought and bled beneath it,—because they
bowed with it upon their toil-worn brows towards Mecca. But
the war-spirit of his ancestors has passed from him, and he takes
to the tented field only on compulsion, and as the last resort,
fighting as one whose soul is lingering behind him among the
soft dreams of his harem and his home.

In drawing the character of our heroine, we must exhibit those
influences which went far towards forming that character, and
we are thus particular because we would show the reader that
it was among such a race that Esmah lived. The soft romance
and delicate thoughtfulness of her disposition received its im-
pressions from the institutions and belongings that wait upon
such a people as we have described. Though born of the fairest slave that the vales of Circassia had ever sent to Constantinople, still she was one of this race, her father's blood was in
her veins, and she had breathed only the air of Turkey.

Save the instruction that she had so aptly received from the
page—and how apt a pupil she was, the reader may easily im-
agine—she had been reared like all other children of the harem.
Her amusements were ever childlike and simple, but, like childhood's self, were all freshness and joy, while her simplest sports
had heart in them. The seclusion to which the strict rules and
habits of her nation consigned her, had debarred her from those
sources of information that the females of other countries enjoy,
and had also shut her out from all the triumphs that youth and
beauty thus obtain. Moving on from day to day in a life of the
most listless and luxuriant inactivity, the eastern female neces-
sarily becomes capricious, and her caprice is dear to her; she

onnects a mystery and meaning with the slightest incident of
.er every-day life. Were a flower that she had nursed and
oved to wither untimely, she would see in its faded stem the
erished beauty of some fond hope. With her, the merest cas-
ialty is pregnant with hidden mystery, and omens and signs
ire taught to her from her earliest infancy. She has but one
iteadily engrossing object, and that is love; aside from this, she
ias no care, no solicitude, and beyond it, she has nothing to
anticipate.

At the hour in which we would introduce the reader to the
gorgeous harem of the Sultan Mahomet, the lovely inmates were
listlessly chatting to each other after the midday meal, sipping
cool and variously colored sherberts, and playing with the roses
and dainty flowers that bloomed in profusion all about the luxuriant and fairy-like apartment. Thoughtless happiness beamed
from the faces there in their careless indolence. Their sensibil-
ities had never been awakened, they knew comparatively nothing of the world, and dreamy glances of passionate love, or
sparkling beams of merriment, were the almost unchanging expression of their eyes, and affording a true picture of the higher
classes of the sex in the East.

Their forms were carelessly bestowed upon the luxuriant
cushions about the regal apartment, and all thoughtless of the
fact, not one of them but presented in her fair and beautiful person, and the easy graceful attitude that nature had dictated, a
model for art. But there was one among the group whose heart
was not with the merry jest or playful feat. Her large, expressive eyes gave token of a depth of thought, and a soft sigh stole
ever and anon from her bosom. The single diamond broach
that closed the gauze about her full and snowy breast, discovered her rank—its value might have ransomed a kingdom!

The wearer was Esmah, the Pearl of the East, as her father
proudly called her, the queenlike daughter of the Sultan.

She sat among the accumulated and fairy-like prodigality of
riches like a queen, outshining in her surpassing loveliness each
sparkling gem that decked her person, and a Persian Jew who
trafficked in diamonds, though they are said to make men mad
by their power, who buy and sell them for a living, would have
turned from the keen sparkling brilliancy of the gem upon her
breast, to the eyes of the wearer, so much more piercing and
beautiful were they. Their dreamy indolence told that the
heart of the owner was far away; she nodded approvingly, per-

haps, now and then, to the soft strains of a guitar that a slave touched lightly for her amusement, or answered vacantly the questions of her fair companions of the harem. And then again, she would fall into a mental sleep, though with her eyes still open to the scene that lay about her.

In this mood one approached her more nearly, yet pausing respectfully lest she should disturb the revery of the princess, but she turned listlessly, and met the new comer with a kind glance, that seemed to say, speak on.

"Art well?" she asked.

" O, yes, very well," sighed Esmah.

" But you seem so absent of late."

"Do I?" she asked, absently.

"Ay, indeed you do."

" Saw you, Esmah, the gallant ambassador that came from the south to-day, to woo thee for the bride of a king?" asked a rosy-cheeked Circassian, of the princess.

" Nay, sister," replied Esmah, for thus they call each other, and indeed all are sisters in the harem.

" Then you should have seen him, sister, for by the beard of the prophet, there is not so handsome a man in all Stamboul."

" Such a superb horseman," suggested one of those nearest the Circassian, as she tipped her fingers daintily with henna dye.

" Superb indeed! and so commanding in figure," said a third.

" Ever since the errand of this new comer was made known, I have fancied that you were more unhappy and melancholy than before, sister," said a young Bulgarian girl, to Esmah, while she picked a cinnamon rose to pieces, and strewed the leaves at the princess's feet upon the soft cushion.

" Nay, it is but a passing vision, sister, that makes me thoughtful; it is nothing more," replied the princess.

"And thou wilt be the wife of a king," said the first speaker, smoothing Esmah's glossy hair away from her clear white forehead, and gazing with undisguised admiration upon the loveliness before her. For the sweetness of Esmah's disposition had won the hearts of them all.

" The wife of a king!" repeated two or three, in admiration.

" Nay, it is not settled upon, sisters," replied Esmah.

"They say there are no harems in Greece, sister, and that women are unveiled to the eyes of the world. Is it not strange, Esmah?" asked the first speaker.

" Custom, sister, alone makes the difference," said Esmah.

"But would you not rather be bride to a rich pasha, and live n Constantinople, Esmah?" continued the Circassian.

"I had rather not be a bride at all," sighed the princess.

"Not be a bride!" exclaimed the Circassian, in astonishment.

"Not be a favorite wife!" exclaimed two or three others, in a breath.

"Yes, sisters, if my heart alone were consulted, I would die as I have lived."

As Esmah said this, she arose, and walking away from the group of fair girls, left them to wonder how it was possible that such a beautiful princess could desire not to be married at all, not even to a king. The princess threw on her yashmac, and passing out upon the green sward, followed the path that led to the bent cypress, where she had so often met the page, and where they had so often exchanged vows of eternal fidelity. How often had she repaired hither alone and to weep!—Her gentle heart had made it her altar of grief, and here she came daily to think of and to weep over the loss of her heart's idol. She had not sat there long musing to herself, before a slight noise was heard in the path, and in the next moment the person of the dwarf was by her side. He drew close to her person, and settling himself upon the ground at her feet, looked up into her face for the sympathy that he never failed to find there. She laid her hand kindly upon his misshapen head, and the poor deformed creature seemed to be happy. It was a strange sight to see so much loveliness and so much of hideousness, side by side.

Brumah, in his rounds of household duty, happening to pass, paused for a moment to look upon the two as they sat there. Upon the dwarf he frowned, as much as to say, you are too intimate with the princess, you have no business here; but to Esmah, he said:

"Still you muse sorrowfully, fair princess; but if I mistake not, there is that in progress which will cheer you up again, and dispel the grief that has so long clouded your brow."

"I have had no grief that I know of, or that you should have noticed," said Esmah, somewhat severely, for she had never borne the chief officer of the household either regard or respect, and in fact most of the inmates of the harem looked upon him more as a jailor than in any other light, for he is literally their guard and keeper.

"True, honored princess; but your solitary strolls in the

garden, and your seeming depression of spirit, led your slave to fear that grief might dwell in your heart."

"We should not judge by outward appearances, Brumah," said Esmah. "Here is this dwarf, with such an unseemly mould; to judge by his make, his spirit must be sour, his mind diseased, and his heart, if he has one, cold and malicious, and yet all this is wrong. He is kind, gentle, and as loving as a child. Appearances are deceptive, Brumah." And as she spoke, she kindly fondled the poor creature by her side, who could only repay her by an eloquent glance of his fine, clear eye.

"True, my honored princess," said the officer, humbly. "Far be it from your slave to suppose you were sorrowful, if such a conclusion be unpleasant to you."

The household officer bowed low, and passed on his way, while Esmah turned again towards the harem. The news that she had heard troubled her mind constantly. Her heart and soul wedded to one whom she could only address in spirit, for she felt that if any entered paradise, it would be such as Alick. Feeling thus, and loving his memory as truly as she had done on the day that his death was reported, how could she but dread the idea of a marriage with any one?

At the door of the harem she met her mother. Rarely had her parent attempted to reason with her upon any subject, or to urge the adoption of any measure upon her child; but now, doubtless, having received direction from the sultan so to do, she opened the subject to her child, showed her the honor that laid in store for her, and marked well Esmah's reply.

"You will consent to the wish of both your father and myself?" asked her mother.

"I will obey you," replied the fair girl, sadly, and with a sigh that came from the depth of her heart.

"Nay, but will you do so willingly, Esmah, of your own free will?" continued her parent.

"Mother," said Esmah, half inclined to fall upon her neck, and weeping there, tell her the secret of her heart, the long-buried secret that had been kept so sacred. But she hesitated; she did not dare to do it, and she merely said, "Your desire is my duty;" and then turned away to sigh alone.

What would Esmah not have given then, for one in whom she might confide, a heart to lean upon, one to whom she might go for advice at such a time? But her mother was not such a person; she could not share in her daughter's feelings, because hey were such as she had never experienced herself, and indeed was hardly able to understand at all, much less to appreciate or sympathize with.

At this moment, a slave entered with a message from the sultan to Esmah, desiring her to repair to his side. She knew the object, and felt like one who goes to receive the sentence of death, for it must prove the death of her future peace of mind.

"In the sight of Heaven, I am Alick's bride," she exclaimed to herself—"how, how can I be another's wife?"

CHAPTER IX.

A HOLIDAY AT THE COURT.

ON the day previous to that on which we have introduced the reader to the harem of Sultan Mahomet, a holiday was given in Constantinople; for a foreign ambassador, accompanied by a large and superbly appointed retinue, came to seek conference with the "Brother of the Sun." Guns were fired, banners displayed, and a myriad of troops paraded before the gates of the royal palace, while the Ottoman fleet thundered forth from its brazen throats in the harbor. Everything was done in the elaborate manner and with the costly elegance of the East. With a treasury at his command only equalled by that of his great rival of Russia, the sultan seemed to pride himself on the liberal display of his wealth.

Amid all the heralding and flourishes of trumpets that might have graced an ancient tournament, the ambassador of Arasilus, king of Greece, was granted audience of the sultan. It was at a period when a temporary peace existed between the two countries, when the latter country was under the protection and support of the Venetians, and the bloody struggle between the Greeks and Turks was for a time suppressed; a struggle that had known little cessation for a period of many years, and which was not long afterwards renewed with increased fury.

The ambassador entered the palace, and walked in the presence of the sultan like one whose noble blood gave him confidence and ease; and a noble specimen of a man he was—so much so that the assembled divan of ministers removed their pipes from their mouths to remark on his distinguished appearance, to each other.   Pipes were interchanged, and the ordinary courtesy of the royal presence duly observed—until the proper moment for speaking.

"May it please your serene highness," said the ambassador to the monarch, "I am deputed by my royal master, to make his highest respect and love to the 'Brother of the Sun,' and to lay his duty at your feet."

"God is great!" said the sultan, "and our royal brother is most courteous."

"Wars and contentions have too long torn our borders, and divided the interests of thy people and his.   He would plant a lasting flag of truce on the dividing lines of Greece and Turkey, and cause friendship to reign forever between the Mussulman and the Greek."

"By the beard of the prophet, you speak well, Sir Ambassador," said the monarch, really pleased with the manner and matter of his words.

"And further, to cement the friendship which he would establish between the throne of Greece and this government, my royal master proposes to ally himself to your serene majesty, by the ties of marriage," continued the ambassador.

This was coming at once to the point, and the speaker paused in thought before he could reply, or commit himself upon the subject.

"Arasilus has heard," continued the ambassador, following up what he seemed to interpret as a favorable expression in the sultan's face, "that you have a child of surpassing beauty, named Esmah, and with her, your serene highness, he would offer to share his hand and throne."

"Has the fame of her beauty reached so far?" he asked.

"Highness, it is known throughout all our kingdoms," said the ambassador.

"It pleaseth us well, for she is the best beloved of our harem."

"Songs are sung in Athens of her beauty, highness; it is said that they were written by the king himself."

"By the king?"

"Highness, yes."

The sultan cast a glance of ill-suppressed pride towards his ministers who heard these words, but said no more; while a slave at a sign from him handed the amber mouth-piece of the royal pipe to the ambassador, a compliment rarely bestowed.

Still the sultan remained silent, until at last he turned to his prime minister, and spoke in a low voice, and afterwards to other officers of state, seated near to his cushions. Then turning to the ambassador, he said:

"The mission you so well represent, is honorable and not unacceptable to us, Sir Ambassador; but upon a point so peculiar and momentous, time is required for deliberation. Stay with us here in our capital, and accept our royal protection and hospitality, until we shall further entertain your business, and prepare ourselves to answer your mission."

"Your serene majesty is most gracious," replied the ambassador.

The presence broke up, and one of the officers of state walked away with the ambassador, upon whom all eyes had been so earnestly bent. He was a man of fine, manly proportions, full in development, and with a native grace and dignity of bearing that commanded respect from all. His face was handsome beyond the cast of most men, and a heavy black moustache shading the expressive lines of his mouth, gave a striking classic appearance to the whole countenance. His hair was black and curly, hanging so bountifully about his neck and face as to form in part a shelter or half mask. His piercing, large black eyes seemed to comprehend everything with which they came in contact, and his gracious expression and language won all hearts to regard him with friendship and interest.

As the minister walked with the ambassador among the beautiful paths of the seraglio garden, they met the dwarf, who, after following their footsteps for some time, came up as they paused, and looked up with his kindling eye into the face of the stranger, and as they seated themselves for a few moments, the poor deformed creature drew near once more, and lying down upon the grass, laid its head upon the ambassador's knee; an affectionate token often practised by an inferior to one above him in Turkey.

"A strange creature," said the prime minister, in answer to a look of inquiry from the ambassador, as he glanced from the minister to the dwarf. "He has been attached to the palace these many years, and is ever fond of thy nation."

"Indeed!"

"Yes, he was kindly cared for by a Greek page, who once served his serene highness, and though that boy foolishly ran away from preferment and home, yet the dwarf has shown great regard for all of thy nation ever since."

" He has a grateful heart; 1 can read it in his eye," said the ambassador.

" Yes, the page once saved his life by risking his own at a fire in the palace, and that is the principal cause of his liking for your nation."

" He is dumb, I should judge."

" Yes; nature, which cast him forth so marred in body, also bereft him of speech."

Thus saying, they passed on to see the lions of the gardens.

The sultan had slept upon the proposition of the Greek king; feuds and wars had ever existed between the two countries. He was himself heartily tired of bloodshed, and thought this a good opportunity to make a settled peace, and place Esmah, his beloved child, in a position eminently above that which she could possibly hold among her own people, where her sex filled a far different sphere from that occupied by them at Athens. Besides, Esmah had for a long period of time been sad and melancholy, ever since the loss of Alick, and indeed was so miserable that the sultan had more than once feared for her reason. He thought that a change of scene might also do her good, as well as further his more worldly designs in accepting the proposal; and thus reasoning, he at length made up his mind to answer favorably the proposition of the ambassador.

It was just subsequent to the hour in the harem, at the time of Esmah's return from the garden and conversation with her mother, that the sultan sent for his child.

" Esmah, my fair pearl, have you heard, through your mother, of this proposition for thy hand?" asked her father, smoothing her soft hair affectionately as he spoke.

" Yes, father."

"And what dost thou think of it, my fairest pearl?" asked the sultan.

" I have no will, father," replied Esmah, resignedly.

" Wouldst be the bride of a king, a southern monarch, who not only marries thee, Esmah, but shares also the honor and dignity of his throne with thee, my child?"

" Thy will, father, is mine," said the gentle girl, still unmoved.

" But, Esmah, I would have thee pleased, nay, I would have thee rejoice at so happy an alliance," continued the sultan.

"Art thou pleased, my child, at so becoming an alliance for thy birth and station?"

" No, father."

" No!"

" I cannot speak falsely," she replied, with her eyes bent upon the floor.

" But wherefore art thou not pleased, my child?" asked the sultan.

" The prophet alone may know, father," replied Esmah.

This was a peculiar expression, and one that precluded all further inquiry. Even to this day it is held sacred in the East; no importunity follows such a reply, be it made to whom it may, before judgment or elsewhere—the prophet once named, and the lips become sealed! no one dares to break the charm!

This custom and observance, though a comparatively unimportant one, is yet most striking in its exemplification of the Turkish character. The simple expression, " the prophet alone may know," acts upon all interrogators like a charm; the head is bowed in respect, and the party queried before, is no longer importuned. So with each national superstitious and mysterious rite, a Turk holds them dearer than his life, and would as soon disregard the one as the other. Esmah could not tell her father the secret that possessed her, for he had never seriously entertained the idea that his child loved the page, and such a revelation to him, even now, might be attended with little less than fatal consequences, and thus she said, " The prophet alone may know."

The truth was, Esmah's heart was as much widowed as though she had been the wife of Alick at the time of his fearful loss, and never could she love another as she would have loved him, nay, as she did love him. The world to her wore a different aspect, the future had no allurements, no attractions; she was indifferent to fate itself, since Alick was no more. If her father desired the alliance referred to, she would not object further. She had said all that a female in her country might say with propriety, and now she felt that she was prepared for the sacrifice if it were necessary.

In this frame of mind, Esmah's heart bled for one confidant, one with whom she might share the grief that oppressed her. She had once a beloved sister, but she was dead now, and buried beneath the funeral cypress. In her longings, Esmah would repair to her lost sister's grave, and strive to hold communion with her spirit there. Beneath those dark groves of cypresses, among the turbaned stones of white marble, she sat often alone. And with the solitary men absorbed in prayer, or groups of women sitting over the graves of departed friends, Esmah felt a secret sympathy that was holy in its prompting. It is a beautiful custom of the East that draws the people so often to the graveyards; here they seem to commune with those who sleep beneath, or supply with water the soft beds of roses planted above their graves. Over their heads are myriads of turtle-doves fluttering among the overhanging branches of the trees, dividing the sway of the gloomy but consecrated place with bats and owls. Byron found stranger interest in a Turkish graveyard, and wrote them down as the "loveliest spots on earth." 'Twas here Esmah's sad heart led her to resort—here that she sought for the sympathy that her soul coveted.

The marriage was publicly proclaimed, and Esmah was informed on the subsequent day to that just referred to, that within the present moon she must be prepared to depart with an escort of honor to meet her future husband, Arasilus, king of Greece; and with the entire submission that is the characteristic of the sex in the East, she acquiesced without a single murmur.

The numberless artificers who came to adorn her person, and to contribute to her peerless wardrobe of jewels and rare costumes, would hardly have believed that they were attiring an unwilling bride, she was so serenely beautiful.

She would have realized as she sat there, with a soft white bosom swelling, and her languid and beautiful eye resting upon the floor, she would have realized, we say, the most extravagant dream of the fancy that had depicted an angel of serene loveliness. But ah! how absent was her heart! How little did she enter into the spirit of her adorning, or realize her own surpassing loveliness! Her thoughts were with the page!

"And now are you not most happy, most to be envied, sister?" asked a companion of Esmah, while she sat thus among her accumulated wealth of costumes, jewelry and costly gems.

But Esmah only smiled a reply. Still the slave continued, little thinking that she was probing the heart of the princess to the very quick:

"You will be so honored and respected, as the wife of a Greek, Esmah, and he, too, a king; and report says he is young and handsome; why, sister, I am sure I envy you."

Another faint smile only answered the well-meant words of the slave, who was busy in examining the riches around them, that had been purchased to grace the bride.

"Say, will you not be truly happy, sister, thus endowed?" continued her loquacious companion, toying with the jewels upon the prisoner's arms and hands, and then leaving them to find fresh beauties in those upon the divans.

"Be *truly* happy, sister!" replied the beautiful girl, sighing deeply. "I have not been happy these five long years."

As Esmah said this, a pearly tear down either cheek attested her heart's deep feeling.

CHAPTER X.

A GRECIAN LADY MACBETH.

AT the time the Venetians possessed themselves of Greece, and fully established their authority at Athens, there was found, among the leading citizens of that ancient city, a family of noble blood, the union being that of a Venetian husband and a Grecian wife. The family of Arasilus, from the fact of its relationship and descent, had abstained from taking any part in the struggles that had existed between the Venetians and the Greeks, and therefore found high favor with the people of the conquering nation. In the course of the arrangement of power and government, the family of Arasilus was raised to the throne, and its head became king.

For a period, fortune vouchsafed peace and repose to Greece, and Arasilus reigned with mildness, and was beloved by the masses of the people. To him there were born two sons, the eldest, a brave, courageous character, the younger, imbecile and weak. In time these sons, too, married, and reared families in Athens. The eldest son, Helotus, was blessed with but one child, while Amarault, the younger brother, became the father of two children, a boy and girl. To the offspring of the elder brother, the throne must in right of inheritance descend, or, in case of his decease, it would fall to the first-born male heir of the younger brother, Helotus and Amarault themselves having deceased.

Already had the old king, their father, gone to his last resting-place, and Helotus, as a matter of course, and in regular succession, assumed the sceptre, and, like his father, reigned to general acceptance. All honors were shared with his brother and his family, and Amarault was made to hold high station in the countenance of the court. But he was espoused to a woman of unbounded ambition—one who never ceased to fill his mind with bold and lofty aspirations, no matter what the means that were necessary to accomplish them, so the object itself were attained. The son of Helotus, now a lad of some three years, was to her a stumbling-block in the way of her ambition. She saw in him the future king of Greece, whereas, if he were dead, her own offspring would wield the sceptre.

It became at once her study and aim to contrive the child's death. She dreamed of it at night, and her waking moments seemed to know no other aim or intent. As we have intimated, her husband was a weak man. Though not wanting in natural power of mind and ability to fill a high station, yet his wife was so masculine, so resolved and determined in her purpose, that he gave way to her in all things, and in the wild schemes which she proposed, he acquiesced almost supinely. Like the wife of Macbeth, she should have been the husband; for, in her restless, daring spirit, she contrived means that stopped not at foul bloodshed itself, for ridding them of the hated obstacle to their son's elevation to the throne.

"It is but a blow, and all is over," said the wife of Amarault to her husband.

"Ay, but such a blow! No, no, wife, I cannot, will not kill the boy," said the husband, with a force that he rarely assumed.

"Shame on thee, Amarault! I will do it then myself, with these hands, if in your manly courage you dare not do the deed," replied his wife.

"I shudder to think upon such a business. If some step must be taken to remove him, let it be done by stratagem, not by bloodshed."

"Fie upon thee for a craven wretch!" said the excited wife. "What! hesitate, when the stake, Amarault, is a throne?"

"We may have the boy stolen away," suggested the husband. "It will be easier done, and far less heavy will it set upon the conscience."

"Stolen away!" repeated the wife, "yes, a pretty trick, and a

trick only. Think you he would not find his way back again?
And worse then would it be than before." ·

" It might be managed so that he need never again return,"
said Amarault.

" If I cannot impregnate thee with some of my own fire and
zeal, then this must indeed be done," was the reply.

This was only one of her attacks upon her husband; but they
were repeated constantly, until his weak nerves and ever feeble
health gave way under the annoyance, and a rapid decline set
in, that soon ended fatally.

Left alone to the management of her ambitious schemes, the
widow of Amarault was at liberty to go to any extreme she
pleased, and with her daring purpose in no way abated, she still
strove for the destruction of the unoffending child of Helotus.
In his unsuspecting generosity, the king mourned freely with
the widow at the loss of Amarault his brother, and vouchsafed
to her a home and support for life. Little did he think that
he was harboring a serpent that should in the end turn and
sting him!

In the managing of her schemes, the artful widow soon realized that she must have some assistant to carry out the purposes
which she should arrange; but it was also very apparent to her
that she must have such a person completely in her power, and
that he must be one of no mean capacity—one such as money
could not buy; and here, for a period, she was at fault. But
finally she resolved upon moulding the father confessor of the
chapel attached to the palace, to her purpose and service. It
was a bold stroke, but what cannot a woman accomplish?

The widow, though possessing a countenance and person that
indicated in some degree the bold and masculine character of
her mind, yet knew full well the worth of modesty and seeming
innocence in a woman, and no one could better assume them
than she, when occasion required. Before the priest she appeared a devout, a mourning widow, and by her constant attendance at the chapel won his interest towards her. Step by
step she did more, and without seeming to do so, yet drew on
the father confessor, who was a man of about her own age, to
declare a passion for her, unholy though it was. This was the
point that the woman had aimed for. Her object was gained.
She drew from the priest a letter, over his own name, praying
her to fly with him and become his wife, in spite of all his holy
ties and allegiance to the church. This was all she wanted.

5

The priest had committed himself and she could ruin him. The truth was, he did really love the widow of Amarault, and this fact gave her still more power over him. She sent for the priest, who came to her private apartments. In the heat of his passion he swore a terrible oath, one so fearful that as he uttered it the priest involuntarily shuddered, and crossed himself with superstitious awe. The oath was, to do whatever she should demand of him, that involved not the taking of human life!

"Ah, lady," said the priest, chilled by the horrible words which he had uttered, "this is a fearful business. I had not thought you capable of such a business."

"Nay, it is of no great harm, so that thou takest care not to break thine oath. Then, indeed, as there is a God in heaven, thou art lost forever!" she said, with a fiendish smile.

The priest trembled with agitation; he began to see the fearful abyss that threatened him, and to realize that such an oath would never have been exacted for any innocent purpose. On the other hand, the woman had studied well his character before she entrapped him, and particularly noted his superstitious nature. She knew that he would fear and regard his oath.

"I have gone too far to recede," continued the confessor. "Let me know the whole. To what does this tend, and what will you have of me that demands such security?"

"Thou knowest well the child of the king Arasilus?" said the woman.

"Well, indeed, for a child who hath nobility written on his brow and in his heart. A sweet, dear boy, upon whom I have ever looked with growing pride—one on whom Greece shall learn to look with mingled love and respect; a child for whom I would do anything that might honorably be done, so much do I regard him."

And this was true, for the priest had by some chance become the most dearly-loved friend the boy knew, sharing with him his little games and sports, and the holy father with him seemed once more to renew his childhood's days. Thus they were much together.

As the priest thus expressed his honest regard for the boy, the widow of Amarault seemed to regard him with a sort of evil joy expressed in her countenance.

"Ha, you love him, then?" said the woman, after regarding him intently for a moment.

"I do indeed love the boy," said the priest, honestly.

"It is well.   You will fit my service *quite* as well as though it were otherwise."

"You speak in riddles, woman," said the priest.

"But you will understand me ere long, I trust."

"What of the boy?" asked the priest, anxiously.

"He is the heir to the throne of Greece," said the woman, significantly.

"True."

"Do you not comprehend me?"

"No."

"Have I not a son also?" asked the woman, looking at the priest meaningly.

"True."

"And still must I speak plainer?"

"Ay—what does this mean?"

"Mean?" said the woman, with a bitter sarcasm, as she repeated his word. "Mean! It means that he must be *removed*. He is in the way! Do you comprehend me now, dull man, or must I speak still plainer?"

The priest seemed horror-struck, and could not reply to her at all for some moments.

"Well," she said, impatiently; "well, what have you to say? Are you prepared to keep your oath?"

"Woman, I understand thee," said the priest, "but our contract, fearful though it be, does not bind me in any matter that concerns the life of a fellow-creature."

"You speak truly, and his *life* must not be harmed, but still he must be removed."

"Go on," said the priest, sighing deeply. "I am bound to do thy bidding, and now let me know the worst! O, holy Father, I deserve this for my sin."

"This boy must be removed," said the woman, "and at once. You may not disappear from court unless you wish it, but he must be placed beyond the possibility of being found, and where he can never return to his home, or Athens. He is young, too young to remember much, and a few years will serve to completely mystify him, and destroy all knowledge of his identity. This accomplished, and you are released from your oath. But let my object be betrayed, either by your carelessness or otherwise, and you not only have the fearful penalty of this oath hanging over you forever, but I will declare your character to the pope and the people, will show your written evidences of guilt, and have you executed."

"I understand you," replied the priest, solemnly, "and with God's help I will keep my oath, more as a penance for my own sin than from fear of thy threat. You say I can remain at court. I desire it not, but shall comply with your demand as soon as may be, and shall also myself leave a spot that must for the future become hateful to me. I am almost ready to thank you for thus opening my eyes, thus turning them in upon myself, thus exposing the vileness of the passion that excited me, and finally thus relieving me from the sinful chain that had fastened about my soul. I now look upon myself in such a despicable light, to think that for one moment I have been absorbed by one like thee, that were I to live for a century to come, I could never forgive myself for the part I have acted. Ah, lady, the beauty and eloquence that Heaven hath so richly endowed thee with, might have been exerted to such noble ends, that even I can grieve as I look upon thee, to see them so sadly, so fearfully perverted. Make known your commands to me in brief, that I may be away and strive to find once more that peace of mind that you have so nearly robbed me of forever."

The priest spoke in sorrow; there was not an angry intonation of the voice that escaped his lips. Had he stormed, the crafty woman would have met him on his own ground; but by the spirit he evinced he had the advantage. She could not speak. Her eyes were bent upon the ground, her bosom swelled with emotion, she seemed trembling with indecision. It was, perhaps, the first moment in all her headlong, mad career, that she had paused to look back. But the evil within her prevailed. She had gone too far, she was fully committed before the priest, and then the object in view had attractions that could not be resisted.

She hesitated but for one moment, then raising her eyes, filled with all the resolution and fire of her will, she said:

"I am resolved, and no earthly power shall prevent the accomplishment of the only object I care to live for."

The widow of Amarault knew her position and power, and, of course, she cared not what motives actuated the priest, so that they did not mar the result of her plans, and she freely told him so, acknowledging the full purpose of her heart.

The priest's romantic dream of love was dispelled like snow

before the sun, and there remained to him only the dark and muddy surface that the white sheet of his imagination had so softly covered with pleasure. He told the woman that she had now done her worst—that she could not add to the task imposed, and that in its fulfilment he should endeavor to make amends as far as possible for the evil that he must commit.

It was a fair summer's evening, a gala day in Athens, and the king had kept open house, and wine flowed like water in his courtyards, where the promiscuous populace revelled in plenty. Feasting and dancing were the order of the day and evening, and the throng made merry and were glad. A cheerful, manly little boy was among them, entering with childish glee into the spirit of the scene, and crowing with delight. He was a sweet child, with his full, clear eye and thoughtful brow, which at times, in the pause of his laughter, assumed an expression of one who had seen experience, and thought deeply.

It was the fair child of the king. On, on it strayed, joining now this group and now another, disdaining all leading or care, and leaving far behind those whose duty it was to look to his wants and protection. At last it approaches the open portal, and is delighted at a display of tiny fireworks just beyond, and rushes towards the bright spot. It was a trick to attract him. That fire was in the hands of the priest, and is extinguished instantly, leaving the bewildered eyes of the child half blind. He is seized in the arms of the guilty confessor and borne quickly off.

We need not describe the consternation that followed the disappearance of the child, nor tell how artfully the widow of Amarault joined apparently in the general sorrow. She feared not that the immense rewards offered by the king for the recovery of his child would lead to the divulging of her guilt; for she knew that stronger influence than that of avarice held her guilty companion in the deed, and she knew full well that he would keep her secret, because it was also his own. Well and carefully had she chosen her victim and slave, and thoroughly had she mastered his character before she resolved upon entrapping him. She felt safe in all her guilt.

Leaving the artful Athenian widow to glory over the success of her scheme, while the greatest consternation reigned at the court on account of the loss of the young prince and heir to the throne, we will go back with the reader to the scene where the sultan's lugger struck the sunken rock and went to pieces on the northern shore of Negropont.

A FITFUL NIGHT ON THE ÆGEAN SEA.

It was a fitful night, that on which the Golden Horn was lost, and the moon seemed as if coquetting with the scene below, now hiding for a moment behind a dark cloud, now peeping out from beneath one less dense, and then shining forth again in unequalled loveliness and purity. The reader will remember that it was during one of those darkened moments when a shroud of black mantled the sea and air, that the fearful accident happened to the lugger. Had the people on board the Turkish frigate been particularly observant, they might have discovered a broad spar like a black speck upon the waters, floating upon the current to leeward after the wreck had disappeared. But their eyes were resting upon the very spot where the sultan's yacht had gone down, without allowing for the strong set of the current to the south, which must carry any floating substance in that direction at the rate of some four or five knots an hour. Had they been thus observant, they might have seen the floating spar referred to, and even, perhaps, discovered and recognized the form of the page secured upon the broadest portion of the timber.

In their blindness and stupidity, the Mussulmen believed him lost with the rest of the ill-fated craft, and returned to Constantinople, and reported the story, as we have already seen.

Alick the page was indeed the only survivor of the Golden Horn. At the moment of the shock, he seized upon a spar that lay along the deck, the one on which the mate had attempted to rig a jigger sail as before described, and upon this he rose to the surface from the vortex of the water caused by the engulfing of the lugger's hull. He was too good a sailor and swimmer not to make the most of his small advantage, and at once secured himself to the best purpose upon the frail support that chance had given him.

On this diminutive spar, the page floated away upon the southern current of the Ægean Sea, with a heart that was very far from being void of all hope. Indeed, he at once calmly examined his position, chose the most secure part of the spar, and reasoned with himself upon the probabilities that succor might reach him, and doubted not that with the break of day he should have floated far out of sight of the Mahomet, and even perhaps fall in with some fishermen of the Archipelago below, with whom he would of course feel at home, and safe from danger.

At last the changeable indications of the weather settled down, and the moon was hidden altogether from sight; a fierce Levanter, as the sailors call it in those seas, set in, and the waves washed at times almost over the page's head; he sat almost constantly with a full half of his body immersed in the water; but with forethought and care, he had already bound himself by a rope that hung from one end of the spar, securely to the centre, and here he buffeted the waves which each moment threatened to engulf and destroy him, with a calm but resolute front.

Once how his heart did leap within him, as he discovered a small fisherman of the isles bearing almost on the same course that he was drifting! They neared each other, but in vain was every effort of the page to excite the attention of the crew, for the darkness of the night hid him from their sight, and his voice was swept far to leeward, until, as he approached the gut of Thecis, the fisherman hugged the coast still more closely, and he was swept further seaward! He did not despair, but his heart almost sank within him as the distance increased between him and the fisherman, but with the native zeal and restless activity of his countrymen, he turned to new schemes and hopes.

O, that was a fearful night which the page thus passed upon the cheerless waters of the Ægean Sea. It would have tried a more manly spirit than his, but a brave heart was in his bosom, and Alick did not despair even for a moment; he breathed a short, fervent prayer, and again devoted himself to take advantage of any incident that chance might disclose whereby he might hope for safety. As morning approached, the Levanter lulled away, and the waves subsided, much to the comfort and security of the page. With the first break of day he found that he had already swept with the current by the classic isle of Scio, and that he was now doubling again with its course away from the shores of Asia towards the shores of Greece.

Now came a moment of intense anxiety with Alick. He knew that the waters rushed with increased velocity by the southern point of the shores of Negropont, on their way to the open sea beyond, and this point he hoped to gain. Indeed, from the isles above he had made his calculations for it, well knowing the set of the current; it now seemed to him to be almost his only remaining hope, and could he effect a landing there, he would be within a few miles of his boyhood's home! How high did his heart now beat with hope! He thought that he could not fail now after all that he had suffered, but it was an Herculean task that he must perform, and one that required, besides a large degree of physical strength, a cool head, and a steady eye to accomplish.

With a small piece of drift wood which he had secured for the purpose, he now endeavored to guide the spar which was swiftly gliding towards the point referred to. He was approaching it fearfully fast, there was no time to be lost; one moment of ill-judged delay might ruin all—cool judgment and intrepidity of action was his only hope. He paused now until he was satisfied that the spar was as near to the shore as the tide would carry it, then recommending himself to Providence, he leaped into the sea and struck stoutly out for the shore.

The page was not very muscular, but his sinews were of an iron stock, and backed by an indomitable spirit, he still had the advantage of the element which he buffeted so bravely. He did not waste his strength by a sudden and nervous struggle, but swam like one who was doing it for amusement only, slowly but steadily, keeping his eye fixed firmly upon the shore, now about a hundred yards distant. He carefully economized every stroke that he made, and drew upon the course of the current all that he could do in safety, until at last, with one powerful and almost superhuman effort, he gained the land but a few feet above the point, which had he passed, death would have been inevitable!

Alick lay upon the shore completely exhausted; he had not the power to move from the spot where he had landed, except to creep beyond the flow of waters. The danger and fatigue of the night, added to the last fearful effort he had just made, were too much for his physical strength, and his energy and mental strength began to decline for the first time; they had been too highly wrought, too severely strained, and the reaction left him indeed prostrate. Here he was discovered by a Greek girl belonging to a fishing hamlet at no great distance, whither he was conveyed insensible.

The kind efforts of the hospitable people partially revived the sufferer; but a few hours, however, had elapsed before a fever set in, caused by the extraordinary efforts he had made, and the physical suffering he had endured. This, no kindness could avert, though it might palliate its course, and the poor page, torn by pains and wrecked in mind, lay there delirious for many long days and nights, his life trembling as it were between earth and the grave. How tenderly did these rude people tend the shipwrecked page, how kindly commiserate with and soothe his wayward mood, and how like an angel looked the young girl whose untiring hand smoothed his pillow both night and day.

Some one has beautifully and truthfully said that no woman can be truly appreciated until she has been seen by the bedside of the sick. There, indeed, does she seem to be in her true sphere; all the tenderness of her heart finds play, all the native gentleness and solicitude of her character shine forth in unclouded brightness. Thus it was with the young fisher girl; her tender heart bled to see such suffering. She prayed in innocence and sincerity for the stranger's recovery, and looked upon his noble brow and classic features with something very akin to love.

Of course, she could not understand the strange mood of his fancy, for much of his talk while in his delirium was in the Turkish tongue. He grieved for Esmah, upbraided the sultan in one breath and blessed him in another, described himself as a base slave, and then regretted that he had sought his freedom at such a cost as the loss of her he loved. Now he was by her side in the seraglio gardens, now pressing her soft, fair hand to his heart, now struggling with the Mussulman who had arrested him as he leaped from the balcony to escape from Brumah, the chief eunuch, and now he was relieved by the well-directed blow given by the dwarf. Once more he was on the deck of his swift-gliding lugger, and the prompt nautical orders issued from his fevered lips. Now he was chased by the Mahomet, now the fight commenced, and the cunning manœuvres followed. Now his fellows dropped dead about him, and the blood covered the decks; his lips were compressed in bitter but stern resolve again, the lugger strikes upon the sunken rock, she sinks, he gasps for breath in his raving, and then rises once more to the surface. Then followed that fearful night on the black waters of the Ægean, and the hope that was blasted when he saw the fisherman bear away from him for the land, and last, his fearful struggle to reach the land, and then exhausted with living over, as it were, all these things again, he fell back almost breathless.

Then would Nydia, the Greek girl, smooth his fevered brow with cooling baths, and gently soothe him to sleep by a soft, low chant of the Greek service. O, it was a dangerous kindness which the young girl did him, for we must inevitably love those whom we serve thus, and her heart was so young, and so unoccupied, that it was already fast filling with thoughts of him who was so noble and so handsome even in the rage of his fever, and the height of his delirium.

One morn, the sunlight, soft and vernal, streamed in at the cottage windows, and lay across the sick page's room. The windows were open to let in the clear, refreshing spring air, and its soft breath revived the invalid as it played across his brow. He breathed freer and deeper of its freshness, and half rising upon his arm, though weak and tottering in the effort, he looked about him like one who awakes from a dream and rouses to assure himself that he is awake. Nydia was by his side; he gazed upon her intently, but with a bewildered look, and said:

"My fair girl, who are you, and what place is this?"

Nydia gazed at him, no less bewildered than he himself appeared to be, for these were the first words of reason he had uttered for many days. It was a moment before she realized that it must be the first dawn of sanity that she had witnessed in the stranger, and she could not suppress a tear of joy, as she said:

"You have been quite, quite ill, sir, and are now getting better."

"Ill?" said the page. "I do feel very weak, but let me see. I was on the water, I think, and swam to the land."

"Yes, that was where we found you, quite exhausted and sick."

"Ah! it is a blank to me since that; has much time passed?"

"It is a month since you first entered our cottage," said the girl.

"So long?"

"Yes, a month yester eve."

"I must have troubled you much in that time, I fear."

"O, no, you have been very quiet all the while," said Nydia.

"And you have watched by me these many days and nights?"
Nydia answered by a simple courtesy, deeply blushing.

"It seems to me now as though I had a faint glimmering of
reason at times since I have been here, and that I do remember
of your thoughtful kindness," said the page. "Alas, I am only
too weak to express my gratitude to you."

"I pray you, sir, do not talk so much; it will weaken you—
and you need quiet very much," said the gentle girl, both endeavoring to turn the subject from herself, and also to care for
the comfort of the page.

"But I will *think* how kind you have been, my gentle nurse,"
said the page, looking the thanks he was too weak to speak.

The page sank back exhausted, and fell into a long, sweet
sleep, that seemed to refresh him more than any he had yet enjoyed, for his mind was no longer struggling in its wild fancies,
and his body was consequently relieved. He breathed so low
and softly, so like a child, that Nydia more than once leaned
over his pillow and listened, almost afraid that he did not
breathe at all; but when he awoke he was like a new man.
True he was weak, very weak, but the eye beamed with reason,
the speech was low, but distinct and musical, and his gratitude
to his young nurse and her kind parents was expressed in such
eloquent and gentle words that they wept over the stranger
they had thus befriended, and bade him thrice welcome to their
hospitality.

"Whence came you when wrecked upon the point?" asked
the father.

"I was wrecked far above," replied the page, "upon the
sunken rock of northern Negropont."

"From so far north?" asked the fisherman, surprised.

"Ay, and floated down upon a spar opposite the south point,
where I swam on shore. I remember nothing after the landing,
except that I felt a dizzy, faint feeling creeping over me."

"You struck the rock where the current makes across the
Ægean from the Dardanelles?"

"Exactly."

"Then you came down the current full thirty leagues and
more."

"It seemed a hundred to me, you may be assured," sighed
Alick, shuddering at the remembrance of that night.

Many days passed before Alick could leave his sick bed, but with such kind nursing he gained rapidly, and after a while strolled out a little way at a time, until day by day he grew stronger, and at last felt himself endowed with his wonted strength and vigor. It was then that he began to talk of parting from his hospitable friends, to whom he had become much endeared. It would be doing him injustice to say that his heart felt quite at ease as to leaving Nydia, the fair fisher girl, who had nursed and tended him with such unremitting kindness. She had been a sweet ministering angel to his wants, and with such a nurse his heart must have been of adamant to remain unmoved.

CHAPTER XII.

THE OLD PRIEST OF NEGROPONT.

ALICK, from the first moment of his return to reason, and of his realization of the fact that he was now on Grecian soil, had experienced the most earnest desire to join his old instructor, the priest, if indeed he was still alive, and therefore it was that he now resolved to bid farewell to Nydia and her kind parents, and seek him. He had no money with which to repay the kindness and hospitality he had so liberally received, but he bethought himself of a diamond broach which bound together his inner vestment. It was a single stone, but of great brilliancy, and, indeed, its intrinsic worth would have richly repaid mercenary services of a much longer period than Alick had been at the cottage. He took the gem from beneath his vestment, and pressed it kindly upon Nydia.

"Take it, my gentle girl, not in payment, but as a token of friendship."

"Nay," replied the mother, interfering, "the stone far outweighs in value our small service; besides, it would be a sin to receive pay for such hospitality to a countryman."

"I offer it only as a token of friendship," replied the page; "take it as such."

Nydia courtesied, blushing, while he fastened her coarse, homespun cape together with a gem that a prince might have coveted.

He embraced the honest old fisherman of Negropont, kissed
the cheek of the mother, and called upon Heaven to bless her,
and, pressing the hand of Nydia to his lips, he left a tear upon
it, as he hastened, with a full heart, away from the cottage.

Nydia remarked that teardrop, and mingled her own with it
freely.

Who could translate the mystery of that tear, or the peculiar
feelings that actuated the breasts of those two young hearts at
that moment? The page felt that had he met with that simple
yet beautiful girl before he had known Esmah, his heart would
have become irrevocably hers, ay, forever; then he felt how
dearly he could have loved her. They had been much together
during his gradual recovery, and Alick had leaned upon her for
support when he ventured out for the first time after his sickness, and he had discovered the depth and purity of her young
heart, all untainted with the world.

Too honorable to raise expectations which he could never
fulfil, the page spoke not to Nydia upon any theme that might
lead her young heart astray. But, alas! though neither knew
it, the page had already made a deep impression there. We do
not mean that Nydia had lost her heart exactly—in fact it may
be doubted if she entertained any more tender thoughts towards
the handsome stranger she had nursed than the page himself
experienced; but there was a fire smouldering in her bosom
that a single word from Alick would have blown into a flame.

It was not to be wondered at, then, that Nydia gazed so
thoughtfully upon the teardrop that wet her hand when they
parted.

But we must follow the page to other scenes, and to dis-
closures that were of startling and most important interest
to him.

Nearly ten years had passed since Alick had left the kind old
priest, who had been to him father, mother, and all, and much
his heart misgave him now lest the old man should have already
been laid in his final resting-place. But he pressed towards the
familiar scenes of his boyhood's days with a swelling heart, and
a tear now and then dimmed his manly eye, as some familiar
object met his gaze, until with the setting of the sun he came to
the humble home of the old priest.

The old man was indeed still alive, but that was nearly all;
for age and arduous study had done their work upon him, and
left their traces in his wrinkled brow and silvered hair, and

every expression told the page that he was fast sinking to the grave. His joy at once more clasping Alick in his arms seemed to know no bounds, and kneeling before the rude cross that stood on one side of his apartment, he prayed long and fervently, after hearing the page's story, for the blessing of Heaven upon one whom it had in its divine wisdom evidently preserved for some peculiar and noble object.

It will be remembered that Alick was a mere boy of some dozen summers when he left the priest. From the earliest his occupations had been such as to absorb his young mind, and quiet any feeling of curiosity as to his parentage. If the subject was ever referred to it was dismissed by the priest with some remark that signified to Alick that he had best not inquire into the matter, and thus the subject was dropped. The boy was too young to place any importance upon the matter of his birth, or, indeed, to feel any great curiosity; but since he had been stolen away into captivity, and learned somewhat of the world practically, he had often longed in secret to know the story of his parentage, let it be what it might.

He now saw the old man sinking fast; he felt that he could not live many days, nay, perhaps not many hours; and he determined to ask him while yet he had power to answer. He did not forget the priest's former answer to his inquiries, and he reasoned shrewdly that he had, perhaps, some good reason 'in which he was himself concerned, why he did not reveal the secret.

"Father," said Alick, "there has ever been one object that has been of intense interest and curiosity to me, growing with my years, and one which you can satisfy."

"Relating to—" said the priest, hesitating, as he drew his hand across his brow, as if to clear away a cloud that had gathered there.

"To my birth, father," said Alick.

"Ah, my son, I had thought to carry that secret with me to my grave."

"Would that be right, father, would it be generous?" asked the page.

"Nay, you know not the circumstances; I fear I shall break my oath, so long, so bitterly kept, but something tells me that I should reveal it now; that the time, the proper time, has come at last when I can speak."

"Ay, father, speak freely, I beseech you, for now I feel more than ever how necessary it is to me to know who, and what I really am."

"First, then," said the priest, "do you forgive me, Alick, from your heart and before Heaven, for the part that I have acted towards you and for what I shall now reveal?" As he spoke he raised himself upon his arm and extended his hand towards the page, who, pressing it, said:

"I forgive you with all my heart, if there be aught to forgive, for you have been very good, very kind to me always."

"Do you freely forgive me all?"

"All."

"Though it shall appear that I have fearfully wronged you?"

"Even then," replied Alick, kindly endeavoring to re-assure the excited and weak old man.

"Kiss this emblem and swear to what you have just said," said the priest, nervously; "it will smooth my way perhaps to Paradise!"

"I swear," said Alick, kissing the priest's sacred rosary.

But the old man seemed hardly competent to the task, for he sank back almost fainting with the exertion that he had already made. A draught of cool water, however, revived him, and after permitting him to recover himself by some minutes of rest, Alick resumed his place by the bedside of the dying priest.

"Speak freely, father," he said, taking the old man's hand within his own.

Gathering his strength for so trying an effort, the priest then told Alick of the feuds of an Athenian house, high in authority, and noble in blood; that there were two heirs to the honors of the house: one, the rightful heir, was motherless, the other, who would attain to the inheritance should the first be removed, was possessed of an artful and intriguing mother, a fiend in the shape of an angel. That woman so coiled herself about him, as he told the page, that he became her slave, and she soon entrammelled his soul with an oath so fearful that even then he trembled to think of it, and for years had been bowed down at heart for the fearful sin he had committed in taking it.

He told the page freely of the part he had played, and of the wiles that had thus entangled and led him on to the committing of crime; he explained those matters already well known to the reader, to the astonishment of Alick.

"And now, Alick," said the priest, solemnly, "know that thy name is *Arasilus! and that thou art the rightful king of Greece!*"

Alick could not speak for wonder. He gazed fixedly, most wildly upon the priest; then he seemed to wonder if the old man had not already become delirious, and approaching with intense anxiety, he asked, almost in a whisper:

"Art mad, old man? have I come only in time delirious?"

"By my hope of heaven," said the priest, "I speak the truth only."

"Heir to the throne of Greece!" repeated Alick in amazement.

"Ay, its rightful king at this very hour," replied the priest.

"Heaven give me strength to meet such tidings as these," said the amazed and bewildered page, almost overcome by the weight of the discovery.

The priest was dying now, and Alick forgot his own interests in the care of the infirm old man. He listened profoundly to the counsel of the priest, which came from his lips so wise and so clear, directing the lost prince what course to pursue, and by what spirit to be governed in his purpose of establishing his rights, that the advice seemed to flow from an inspired source, and Alick felt it to be so. And now lifting his emaciated hands towards heaven, the last breath of the old man passed away in a blessing upon the young page's head.

In all communities there is a class of people restless and uneasy by nature, who gladly hail any change with delight, be it either for good or bad. This class of the populace of Athens threw high their caps, and shouted, "Long live Arasilus!" when it was made known that the young prince, who had been so long missing, had returned to claim the sceptre of Greece; but wiser men, courtiers, and the council of state, moved with more deliberation, and carefully examined the documentary evidence that the priest had amply furnished, with his confession, and other indisputable papers.

Had they needed other proofs of the identity of the prince than the documents he had produced, they might have read it on his clear brow, in his full dark eye, and in his noble bearing. Indeed, many exclaimed with admiration and astonishment, as he rode into the palace gate to be formally reinstated to his rights, "Fore Heaven, how like his father!"

The artful widow of Amarault was dead; she did not live long to see the consummation of wishes that had cost her so dearly to accomplish. Her son, but a weakly and fragile person, in mind and body, seemed to rejoice at the return of his cousin, *lly* it would relieve him from the cares and annoyances of the throne. The contrast between the two but rendered Arasilus the more popular, for he looked the king in every motion. He was crowned in triumph, and welcomed back to the court with regal honors and celebrations.

We say that the cousin of Arasilus seemed to rejoice at his return; at least he said he was most happy to resign in his favor, and relieve himself of the cares and importunities of state, besides complimenting his cousin as being far better adapted to fill the throne than himself; but he spoke dishonestly; no such thoughts dwelt in his heart. The truth was, he at once saw that the best course for him was to yield his position gracefully, making a virtue of necessity.

"Cousin, remain by us, and share the honors of our throne, and let us learn from thee, who hast filled this high station so long and well, how best we may win equal credit as exponent of the laws."

"Thanks, noble cousin," replied the dissembling noble, who was outwardly all blandness and courtesy, while his heart was full of gall and bitterness; and accepting a seat at the right hand of the king, he strove to impress upon the people at the coronation of Arasilus that he was still next to the throne, though another filled it.

Thus the two cousins settled down, the friends of each other, at least to all appearances, and Arasilus certainly accredited Amarault for all he protested, and trusted him freely in all things, and sought his advice in relation to matters that constantly came before him.

Arasilus had seen too much of life already; he had endured too much of hardship, and seen too much of adversity and disappointment, not to be somewhat of a philosopher, even at his age, and therefore, all the splendor that surrounded him, and all the honor that waited on his steps, did not change him at all. He was the same calm, collected and manly spirit as before, governed by the same honest dictates of the heart. Unlike most men, prosperity had not spoiled the sultan's page, who now wrote himself king of Greece.

The first secret glow of joy at his good fortune brought with it the memory of Esmah to his heart, and in spirit he shared it with her. In every arrangement his purpose and aim bore upon his hope of one day enjoying it with the object of his young and ardent love; and though far away, and surrounded by circumstances that might render the hope of a future union almost unreasonable, still he hoped on, as true to her as when he sat by her side under the bent cypress, in the seraglio gardens.

The principles of the Mussulman's religion prohibited the intermarriage of a Mahometan with a Christian. This no one knew better than Arasilus; for, when an humble page, he had often talked of this fact with Esmah. This seemed an almost insurmountable barrier to him, and he passed a long period in endeavors to overcome it, but still time went on, and news reached Athens that a mixed marriage, as it was called, had been sanctioned by the sultan. A Christian and a Mahometan were united, though both were directed to withdraw at once from Constantinople.

Arasilus saw the principal stumbling-block that had impeded his way now removed. He could propose a union to the sultan, without the fear of its being construed into an intended insult, and he resolved to do so through a trusty and discreet ambassador, representing his policy and desire to be that of a union that should insure future peace between the courts. He did not propose to make himself known to the sultan as his former page, lest it should in some way mar his plan. And with this purpose his arrangements were made, though not until some five years subsequent to his escape from the sultan's service, owing to the force of circumstances and the occurrence of matters beyond his control.

It was on this service that the Greek ambassador was sent, as we have represented him, at the court of the Brother of the Sun; it was on the occasion of his arrival that the fair inhabitants of the harem rallied Esmah, and the reader is aware how the proposition of the Greek king was received by the sultan.

Thus we bring the reader even with the plot of the tale, and he will not wonder that Arasilus, king of Greece, should sue for the hand of the sultan's beautiful daughter, Esmah, "The Pearl of the East."

CHAPTER XIII.

THE ASTOUNDING DISCLOSURE.

THE fair moon was lighting up the oriental picture that surrounds the seraglio gardens, and prying in among the mosques and palaces, the pleasant walks, dark cypresses and bubbling fountains, when Esmah stole out for one parting reverie upon the spot rendered sacred to her heart by a thousand remembrances. Her steps were turned towards the bended cypress where she had so often met the page, and where they had last parted from each other. Slowly and sadly she pursues the path, musing on the past, and the new scenes that must open with the future, for to-morrow she would leave Constantinople forever.

Is that dark shadow on the edge of the path cast by her slender person? Nay, it is the dwarf, slowly stealing along in the shade, to join the princess at the spot he knows full well she will seek. How uncouth his figure, and how strangely he moves, helping himself on, with either hand placed on this side and that, with a hump upon his back like a camel. But all the while his soft, tender eyes are bent upon Esmah—how plaintive in expression, how devotedly they rested there; rendered more beautiful from the deformity of their poor owner's person, those eyes seemed as if left for a redeeming token that the *soul* was not deformed.

She sat her down upon the same seat that the page and herself had occupied together five years before. How her bosom heaved, for she knew that she was there for the last time. She could almost hear her own heart beat, it was so still around, and the memories of the past crowded so thickly upon her. The moon that had fairly risen, blazed forth over the hills of Stamboul, and the sleeping city of Mahomet; long shadows were drawn across the path, and Esmah felt a sort of superstitious awe stealing over her, she knew not why. She had been here at as late an hour a hundred times; but her mind perhaps was nervous and weak from grief and excitement, and the knowledge that she was bidding these scenes farewell, probably forever. See how she starts at that moving shadow! But she recovers again from her tremor, as the dwarf approached and coils himself at her feet. She seems to find fresh emotion even, in looking upon him, for he was loved and cared for by Alick, and was devoted to the young Greek. She lays her hand kindly upon his head, and the poor thing looked up into her face with unutterable gratitude. With only her to love in the wide world, how much even the dwarf could love his mistress.

At this moment Esmah heard footsteps approaching the spot. She was the more surprised at this, because of the lateness of the hour, and also because of the sacred character of the place; but still she heard distinctly the gentle tread of approaching steps. The dwarf, too, had discovered the approach of some one, and Esmah saw his long bony hand grasp a broad blade in his bosom. She felt no fear; she knew the dwarf could protect her, if necessary; for, though misshapen and seemingly clumsy, he was as quick as thought when there was occasion.

A tall shadow crossed the path, and Esmah saw, slowly nearing the spot, the ambassador who was her father's guest, and with whom she was to depart on the morrow. How he could find access to this part of the gardens she knew not, but felt reassured at the discovery, and even the dwarf had resumed his apathy, and seemed content. She had only seen the ambassador at a distance, and had not yet been introduced to him, but presuming that he would pass by the spot without noticing her, she determined to wait for him to do so, and then to retire. But the ambassador, having discovered her, seemed inclined to speak, and drew still nearer to her seat with a respectful bearing and a low obeisance.

"The princess Esmah chooses a romantic spot, and a lone hour for her meditation," he said, blandly.

The princess started again, and looked about her, as though some strange remembrance had suddenly come over her, but collecting herself, she replied:

"I was bidding these familiar scenes a long farewell; for I go to-morrow, my father tells me, to meet my husband in Greece."

"True, lady, and I have the honor of having been selected by my sovereign, to perform the sacred duty of your escort."

Saying which the ambassador looked about him inquisitively,

as though to see if they were observed or liable to intrusion, and then said:

"We are well met, fair princess, here alone; for I am instructed by my royal master, to seek such a meeting as this, unheeded and in secret, and to demand of thee, upon my truth, if thy heart is free and untrammelled; for he would not possess a hand without a heart."

"Indeed!" said Esmah, surprised at this apparent generosity.

"It would ill become my royal master to espouse thee, fair princess, with the hope of enjoying the richness of thy love, and the entire wealth of thy heart."

"You speak well, sir."

"Then will it please thee, lady, to unveil thy heart to me, as as to him, who, through me, has sought thy hand in marriage?"

"I can see no harm in speaking truly," replied Esmah, thoughtfully.

"Then, is thy heart free, lady?" asked the ambassador.

"From all earthly ties, yes," replied the princess, sadly.

"You have never loved, then?" continued her interrogator.

"Yes."

"Then why is not one so high and noble as thou art, espoused to the object of thy affection?" asked the ambassador.

"Heaven hath willed it otherwise," she answered, sadly.

"Hath the sultan intervened between thee and thy love?"

"Nay, a higher power even than that of my father."

"Was it the hand of death, lady?" asked the ambassador.

But Esmah seemed dreaming—lost for the moment with herself, and answered not the query addressed to her. Seeing her absence of mind, the ambassador, after a moment's silence, spoke again:

"The object of your affection sleeps, perhaps, beneath the cypress of St Sophia?"

"Or, rather, beneath the waves of the Ægean Sea," replied Esmah, sighing.

"If he be dead, is not thy heart free, free as before, lady?"

"It is free, but never can it love as it has done," replied the princess.

"I trust you will not hold me inquisitive beyond propriety, but I ask, lady, if he whom you did love was noble and of rank?"

Esmah seemed again to have forgotten herself in her memory of the past, and now, as she turned to answer this last inquiry of the ambassador, enthusiasm and love swelled her heart, and she seemed to forget that she was speaking to one who was to her a stranger.

"Noble," said she, "as Heaven can make, but humble in blood and fortune. He was my father's page, sir. I fear it is unmaidenly for me to reveal to thee, but to my own kin I cannot do it. He was of thy people, a Greek. I was a young and wayward girl, thoughtless and trifling, when he taught me day by day to turn my eyes within myself. He taught me, too, his religion and the language of his native land, and by raising me in mental culture above those about me, he isolated me from my companions, and rendered his own society more dear to me. We grew up from childhood together, and the first time he saw me, he saved my life in the waters of the Bosphorus. Do you wonder, sir, that a Turkish girl, who had seen little beyond the walls of the harem, should love with her whole soul such a being as my father's page?"

"I cannot gainsay you, lady," replied the ambassador, much moved by the tender eloquence he had heard from her beautiful lips. "Indeed, your love was but natural."

"Thank you, O, a thousand times, for it was natural. Heaven had made him in the express image of itself; he was very, very noble in person."

"And was he worthy of thy love, was he constant and true to thy faithful heart?" asked the ambassador.

"As the needle to the pole. He was ever with me, ever thoughtful, ever kind; and his joy seemed to be, mostly, how he might serve me most acceptably, how best evince the love that filled his heart."

"I know he must have been worthy, or else he could never have impressed thee thus," he replied, earnestly.

"Ah, sir, you are a Greek, and can sympathize with me. I am very glad that we have met thus, and can speak without restraint, for long has my heart yearned to reveal its heavy secret."

"Then for these many years you have been true to his memory?"

"His name has been in my nightly prayers for five years."

"Then behold him once more, dearest," said the pretended ambassador in his natural tone of voice!

As he spoke he threw back the thick clustering hair from his forehead and temples, and tossed off his cap that she might the better recognize him.

" Alick! Alick!" cried Esmah, falling in a swoon at his feet.

The dwarf recognized the page in the ambassador as soon, and with the speed of the wind rushed away at a sign from him, for water, which soon revived the fair creature, whose head now rested upon the breast of her long lost and dearly loved Alick. Nearer and closer the dear girl pressed to his side, and closing her eyes again, like one, who, waking from a pleasant dream, strives to woo back the sweet delusion that wakefulness dispels. It was long before either spoke; their hearts were too full, they were far too happy to speak. The almost distracted dwarf now came to press the lost one's hand to his lip, and then rushed away to the very end of the long path, as though he could find no vent for his delight except in violent exercise.

" But thou art only found, dear Alick, to be lost again; for you are to convey me to Athens to be another's bride. O, I cannot leave thee again!"

" That is a trick only, for thy father and the court," he replied.

" A trick, Alick? I do not understand you," said she.

" Ay, I am no ambassador, Esmah, and yet I am in one sense an ambassador, too," replied he, " but I am striving for your hand, incognito."

" What mean you, dear Alick?" asked Esmah, innocently.

" That thy lover is the king of Greece," said he, smiling.

" That I knew before," replied Esmah.

" Wilt not understand, dearest?" said he, playfully chiding her. "Am I not thy lover, thy true lover? and am I not Arasilus, king of Greece?"

" Thou, Alick?"

" Even so."

" My father's slave a king!"

" Arasilus, and none other."

" You are not jesting?"

" Indeed, I am most serious."

" I am all amazement," replied the young girl, almost weeping.

" But none the less happy, Esmah!" he said, tenderly.

Surprise rendered the fair girl dumb. Then Alick told her of his escape from the wreck of the lugger, and his arrival at the southern point of Negropont. How he had been ill, and kindly cared for, for many long weeks, and finally of his finding his old protector and instructor, the priest. He revealed to her the treachery that had deprived him of his rightful inheritance. All this seemed to her like some fairy tale, but she knew that

Alick would not deceive her, and she wept and smiled by turns.
It was a strange meeting, that of the king of Greece with the
sultan's daughter in the seraglio gardens.

Arasilus, for thus the reader must know him in future, explained to Esmah why it was important that he should not be
recognized as the former page of the sultan; indeed, both saw at
a glance that it might be the means of breaking the compact
already so nearly consummated, and therefore it was agreed
upon that both should maintain the most profound secrecy as
to the events that had just occurred, and that they should meet
at the proper time for the introduction on the morrow, as strangers to each other. In the meantime Esmah would hurry back
to her apartment in the harem, and prepare herself for the
coming journey.

"Till then, Esmah, farewell and after to-morrow that shall be
a word that we will never repeat to each other," said the pretended ambassador, kissing that dearly loved hand, and once
more gathering about him his dress and assuming the dignity of
his pretended office.

Arasilus, taking advantage of his former knowledge of the
secret passes of the palace, and more particularly of a postern
gate that he had himself constructed, in the hope of one day im-
proving it to his advantage, found no trouble in obtaining an
entrance to the garden, and the spot where he had met with
Esmah—but he believed that no little caution was still necessary
to effect his object.

A sign brought the dwarf to his side. The poor mute spoke
not, nor could he understand the meaning of words to any purpose. But Alick had always been able to make him comprehend his wishes with the utmost facility, and now easily signified to him that it was necessary for his safety that he should
remain unknown. The intelligent eye of the dwarf answered
for his speechless tongue, and Arasilus was satisfied of his
discretion.

It was not to be wondered at that the former page, with five
years added to his life, and with a marked change in the wearing of his hair, besides the increase of a black and huge beard,
added to the entire change of character and being, should not
be detected as the former slave of the sultan. Besides, was not
the page drowned in the Ægean Sea? The probability is, he
might have appeared at Constantinople in almost any character,
and he would never have been recognized.

Elaborate were the ceremonies that were performed in the sultan's mosque, in giving over Esmah to a Christian husband, and sad were the forebodings of many good and true Mussulmen at the sacrilegious act against the Koran, of which the sultan was guilty.

Before meridian that day, the cortege passed through the city walls on their way to Adrianople, from whence they would embark for Greece. The sultan almost wept with joy to see the unaccountable life and animation that beamed from the face of his fair daughter, the first time for years. Her companions of the harem kissed her with feelings of secret awe, for the change was so great in her looks and spirits, that they declared that the prophet, for some good purpose, had wrought it. None guessed that Alick the page, the noble and courtly ambassador, and Arasilus the king, were the same!

CHAPTER XIV.

TWO HUMBLE LOVERS.

SOFT and fair is the evening on the island of Negropont; the setting sun has tinted the current of the Ægean Sea with a deep red, and it makes around the southern point of the island, at the twilight hour, like a river of blood. Back from the shore, at a distance of less than a mile, was one of those snug but humble cottages, that make the homes of the fishermen of the Grecian isles. In a grove near by walked two persons enjoying the bland air ladened with fragrance that was wafted from the country beyond. They were engaged in earnest conversation, and evidently the subject was one of deep interest. One, a young man of fine and pleasing exterior, whose countenance was glowing with enthusiasm—presented a fit model for a sculptor. His face was handsome, and his bearing manly, yet tender to the girl by his side. She might have been two years younger than her companion; small in figure and possessing a sweet form and being, so unaffected and naturally lovely, that you would have paused in admiration at her appearance.

It required no prophet's eye to decide that they were lovers, but to the reader one is already known; it is Nydia the fisher girl. Alazar was the son of a neighboring fisherman, and had known her from her earliest youth, but never until now had he declared in plain language his love for the beautiful and innocent Nydia. She knew not the art of coquetry, and answered his tender proposition with honest simplicity.

"Alazar, it would be untrue in me, if I denied that your love is returned, but, alas! what have we, two young, inexperienced persons, without means, to do with marriage? I know that it seeems heartless to refer to such things, but you remember one or two instances of such alliances in our own isle, Alazar, when misery and want have been the sad result."

"Though love can but poorly heed such matters, Nydia, still I love thee only the better for this providence and forethought. Only assure me that your heart is mine, and I will work cheerfully years, to lay by a store that shall serve for our union and support. Our wants are humble, and my arm is skilled and strong; we could be comfortable on little of the world's goods."

"True, an thy health be spared, Alazar, and no misfortune befall us."

"Against this unknown future, Nydia, then will I provide, and with the dear assurance that you have given me, it will be a cheerful task," replied the happy young sailor.

The fair girl smiled her approbation as they turned towards her father's abode.

"Alazar, have you noticed the felucca yonder?" asked the old fisherman.

"Until the moment, no," replied the young seaman, with some curiosity.

"I should know most crafts of her tonnage that might be found between Candia and the Dardanelles, but she comes from below Malta or the Ionian Isles."

"But what can such a felucca be doing hereaway?" asked Alazar.

"Ay, that's what puzzles me; she's too light for a trading vessel, and too poorly equipped for a smuggler or a corsair. By our lady, but she seems tacking for our coast!"

The fisherman spoke truly; as there floated a little to the north of the isle of Scio a small felucca-rigged craft that had stood thus far north against the current, and now, after allowing for the southerly drift, was evidently bent upon making a harbor on the shores of Negropont. She was of humble size even for a fisherman, but what puzzled the father of Nydia and the young seaman whom he addressed, was to know what business could bring the stranger in that direction. For men of their class were so well posted up in nautical matters, that they could read a vessel's business as well by a sight at her running gear, as a midshipman could by a look at her manifest; besides they knew everything that floated in the Archipelago, unless it were vessels of the long voyage, ships that came through the Straits of Gibraltar, square-rigged, and generally wearing the cross of St. George.

Unable to classify the felucca, the two watched her with a suspicious eye until she was safely moored near by their own fishing crafts, when a small boat, pulled by a couple of seamen, and containing a third in the stern, hauled up to the landing. He in the stern leaped on shore, and, giving some orders to the other two, who pulled back to the felucca, he approached the spot where Nydia's father and Alazar stood watching his movements.

The new comer was dressed in the costume of a Greek seaman, but rather more elaborately than those whom he now approached. He wore high top boots, a heavy leathern belt, and a large buckle to hold it in place. The belt supported a pair of pistols and a heavy hanging blade, such as was worn in those days by masters of trading crafts in the Mediterranean. His hair was slightly tinged with gray, and his face was bronzed to that dark hue which the exposure of years to the sun produces. There was an easy, jaunty air about the stranger, however, that showed he had seen some good society in his day, and he bore a manly eye and generous expression upon his face.

"A fair night to you, friends," said the new comer, approaching. "Is this not Negropont?"

"It is, most surely," replied the old seaman. "You must be a stranger in these seas."

"True. I was making my way up to Corfu in the Marmora, and thought it would be best to lay by for the night. Could I get lodgings on shore?"

"I have a cottage and a bed, to which you are welcome," replied Nydia's father, though, truth to say, the old fisherman himself disliked the idea of inviting the stranger to his board.

"Thanks, old man; you are as hospitable as the heart could wish. Why this realizes the stories of olden time. You take in a stranger as if he were an old friend."

"We are taught here in Negropont to hold every man our friend until he proves himself our enemy," said the fisherman.

"Good, again," said the stranger. "It is weary staying so long on board, and all the while in sight of land, and so I shall accept your generous offer."

"Do you come from the Ionian coast?" asked Alazar.

"Yes, bound, as I told you, to Corfu, on special business," replied the stranger. "You are principally fishermen here, I judge—a thrifty and honest calling."

"Honest, sir, but as to thrift," said the old fisherman, "we manage to live, and that is all."

"But we are told that you draw heavy nets here in your archipelago of isles, and that a short season supplies you for a year's comfort."

"Those speak unwisely who utter such words," said the old fisherman. "Our business, though unlike the crops, it rarely fails altogether, yet affords but a meagre livelihood at least."

"But your industry makes up for that, I dare say. Now there is as smiling a cottage and as sweet a home as a prince could show, had he half the wealth of the Indies."

As the stranger spoke he pointed to the home of Nydia's father.

"It is a *happy* home," said the fisherman, joyfully, with a tear in his eye as he looked with honest pride at his lowly cottage.

"I know it," said the stranger, frankly; "it is written upon every flower about its door."

His words, so tinctured with honest admiration and truth, soon made them feel at home in his company, and to address him with welcome feelings, and richly to enjoy his fluent tongue and cheerful conversation.

Thus chatting pleasantly, and upon themes that drew out the old fisherman's pride and pleased his vanity, the stranger walked on towards the home of Nydia, where they entered; and as Alazar and Nydia, and her mother, father, and the stranger approached the board, the old fisherman, crossing his arms upon his breast, uttered a short but sincere offering of thanks to the Giver of all good gifts. The stranger imitated his humble host, and listened with profound reverence depicted upon his bronzed countenance, and then partook of the rude but cleanly fare set before them, with an appetite so ravenous as to be remarked by even the good mother and the host.

After the repast, all joined in the universal pipe, while the stranger told many pleasant stories of adventures and experiences of the world that charmed the humble people. To the old man he made some interesting remarks touching the interests of the fishermen in the new laws of Greece, with which he was thoroughly conversant; to the mother he talked of matters that pleased and interested her, and to Nydia and Alazar he told stories of romantic adventures and successful love, that absorbed their hearts in the issue. The hours sped on, but they heeded them not, for it was not often that they were so entertained.

At last he called Nydia one side, and told her that he had already studied her heart, and found that she loved the young fisherman who sat then by her side. He talked to her so gently, so wisely, and evinced such real interest in her fate, that she blushingly acknowledged that what he surmised was true, and that herself and Alazar were already betrothed to each other.

"And is there any impediment to your union, my good girl?" he asked.

"None, save that a few years must intervene," replied Nydia.

"And why so long a delay? You are both of goodly age," said the stranger.

"True, but Alazar is poor—he does not even own his boat yet."

"Ah, that is it; and yet your parents consent, I suppose?" he asked.

"They have never objected," replied Nydia, smiling at his earnestness.

"My honest fisherman," said the stranger, turning to the father, "you know no objection I suppose to the union of these young people?"

"None, when Alazar shall be able to promise my daughter a competent support."

"Very good, that part I will see to; and as an earnest of my sincerity," said the stranger, producing from beneath his vestment a purse heavy with gold, "there are two hundred golden ounces, a dower for you, my gentle and worthy girl."

All started in amazement at his words, for two hundred ounces was more money than any one there had ever seen before, or, indeed, had ever expected to be worth in the world.

"Nay," said the stranger, smiling at their amazement, "sit down and listen to a short story that I have to tell you, and then, perhaps, you will not wonder at this small gift, which I am so happy to make this worthy child."

"The story I am about to speak of, I have from undoubted

authority,—I may say from the lips of the very person referred to. Some six years gone by, one morning there drifted on shore, at the southern point of this island, a poor Greek youth, who had but lately escaped from servitude among the Turks at Constantinople. He was faint, wearied, and, indeed, almost at death's door from exposure and exhaustion; but as he lay there panting upon the sand, a young girl discovered and befriended him. He was brought to her father's cottage, where a burning fever set in.

" Wild and delirious, this young Greek tossed upon his restless bed for more than a whole month, but night and day the young fisher girl tended him like a sister, unwearied, uncomplaining, denying herself the necessary sleep that nature required, in order that she might minister to his simplest whims, and smooth his fevered pillow. Well, in time the sick one recovered, slowly, and still dependent upon the kindly support and aid of his gentle, self-sacrificing nurse, until finally called by imperative duty, he bade her, and the hospitable roof that had sheltered him, farewell.

" I see that you all recognize the picture, and that you remember the poor, shipwrecked youth whom you so generously befriended. Nay, I can even discover tears in your eyes at the simple but honest relation which I have given you, for, in your self-sacrificing hospitality, you only looked upon the service you rendered as a duty, nor reviewed it in the light in which I have shown it to you."

" We do remember the noble young Athenian, who escaped so miraculously from the bloody Turks," said the father, dashing away a tear as he spoke. " But the credit that you would give us for so small a service is undeserved, for who would not have done as much for a fellow-countryman ?"

" You should know," said Nydia, with deep interest, " what became of him afterwards; we have never heard of him since."

" He stands before you!" said the speaker, throwing off the wig he wore, and wiping away the nut-brown dye that had been placed upon his face to change its color.

The surprise of that little party can hardly be depicted in words. The happy congratulations that followed were so sincere and unaffected, that it seemed almost a sin to end them. The purse was forced upon Nydia, and the promise of a handsome gift to both her and her parents, and the happy young sailor. Alazar could not find words to express the gratification that he felt, or his thankfulness to the man who had enabled him to overstep the space of years, and marry his beloved Nydia within the month. The father grasped his hand with honest regard, and besought Heaven to bless one who had so long remembered a single act of hospitality, and so generously repaid it again.

"Nydia, I think even Alazar will not object to my imprinting one pure kiss upon that lovely brow, a brother's regard prompting it."

As he thus spoke, Alick pressed his lips to her forehead and said:

"May your future life be as happy as I have often prayed it might be since we parted, and may its pathway be illumined by the constant rays of peace. The poor invalid never forgot his gentle and lovely nurse, and her name has been often the burthen of his prayer."

Nydia blushed deeply.

"Has he been sometimes remembered, my gentle girl," whispered Alick.

"Indeed, indeed he has," she replied; "and I shall never forget the pleasant hours that we passed together while you were recovering day by day from your sickness."

"My gentle nurse," said Alick.

He felt the hand tremble within his own! Perhaps Nydia remembered the single tear that he left upon her hand at parting; perhaps she recollected the feelings that had so nearly blossomed in her heart. But be it as it may, he read a deep and earnest response to his words in those beautiful eyes, that it were worth a pilgrimage to realize.

"But stay," said the father; "even now we know not whom we thank. My good friend, you surely will not withhold from us the name of him to whom we owe so much, who has returned our humble kindness forty fold."

"It would not help the case, believe me," he replied.

"And yet after this pleasant re-union," suggested Nydia, "it would be most agreeable to know who befriended us."

"True."

"And will you not then tell us?" she asked, with an arch smile.

"Surely you can have no object in keeping your name a secret from us now," said the father.

"No, my object is gained. I have no further cause for disguise. I wished to see you once, as I had formerly seen you, to learn how best I could serve you. This I have accomplished, and shall take good care to strengthen by renewed and proper gifts."

Then throwing open the rough coat that covered his inner vestment, he said:

"I am Arasilus!"

All gazed for a moment at the glittering star of royalty that blazoned upon his breast! and then kneeling, exclaimed in one voice:

"It is the king!"

CHAPTER XV.

THE QUEEN OF GREECE.—A HEARTLESS PLOT.

THE lapse of some three years brings us to Constantinople once more; the superb, peculiar, incomparable capital of the Ottoman empire, with its chaplets of swelling cupolas, and groves of slender minarets, its avenues of glittering porticos and palaces, the glorious Bosphorus, the fairy-like seraglio, the lovely suburbs, besprinkled with valleys and streams, and its sea-beat shores, dotted by myriads of caiques, shooting hither and thither like fire-flies in the air, all still the same.

Arasilus has been summoned to the sultan on matters of grave import, touching the relation of the two countries; and placing his cousin on the throne, to fill that seat for him until his return, he bade farewell to his dearly loved wife, the beautiful Esmah. He departed from Athens and came now to answer the summons of Mahomet, the Brother of the Sun. Leaving Arasilus to arrange his business at the Turkish court, we will in the meantime return to his wife, and the house he had left.

If Esmah was lovely when first introduced to the reader in the sultan's palace, how much more so was she now, with all the elegance of ripened womanhood, with the soft and gently-subdued air, that perfect control and unruffled happiness impart? These charms, added to all her early beauty of person, rendered her almost too lovely. In her noble lord's absence, she remained almost in utter seclusion, admitting only her sacred confessor to her apartments.

Some three years had passed since Amarault had abdicated in favor of his cousin, and though in the mean time he had been treated with distinguished honor, still there had grown up in his heart bitter hatred towards Arasilus. First, because he felt that he had been the means, though innocently, of deeply wronging him, and secondly, because his noble cousin was so much more honored and beloved, as king, than he had ever been. Besides this, he envied him the love and companionship of such a sweet being as his wife, and feeling thus, his spirit to do him evil was only augmented by the opportunity that was afforded him to execute it, since he filled a second time the throne while Arasilus was called away to the court of the sultan.

By the most insidious wiles he endeavored to ingratiate himself into the heart of Esmah. He was of course admitted to her society, being reigning king, and her husband's cousin. He shrewdly studied the fair lady's character, and knowing that she must be attacked in no common way, he made the subject of his study how best to deceive, and perhaps even to dishonor her. Thus could he gain a double purpose; the gratification of his own passion, and the ruin of Arasilus's peace of mind and happiness forever. He sat with her alone, talked much of her absent husband, a subject that delighted her, praised him for his noble nature, his administration of authority, and referred to a hundred themes that complimented her absent lord, until Esmah began each day to look forward to his visits with pleasure.

Step by step Amarault approached his fell purpose, until a propitious moment arrived, when he shocked the pure and tender heart of the queen, with a proposal so black that she was struck dumb. She could not even denounce him in so bitter terms as she should have done, nor express the indignation that filled her breast.

"Have a care, lady," said the villain; "if you banish me hence, you make an enemy who will be revenged on you and yours, though it cost him his life."

In her proud indignation, she vouchsafed not a word, but with a dignity that made even Amarault quail before her flashing eye, she pointed towards the door of the room, for him to leave it on the instant. Nothing but stern indignation was depicted on her face while he was present; but when he had gone, and she was left alone, her woman nature burst forth, and throwing herself upon a couch, she covered her face with her hands and wept like a child, partly in anger, and partly in grief, that she had been so insulted and deceived.

Esmah thought long and sorrowfully upon this event, and trembled as she remembered one remark of Amarault's, that he would be avenged upon her and her lord too. She feared that some trap would be laid for Arasilus by his wily cousin, who now had a double object in view, that of gaining the throne once more, and his own safety; for she reasoned that he would expect her to reveal his insult to the king, who would be sure to punish it with the severity it merited. The thought of any danger occurring to her husband made Esmah almost crazy to think upon, and she hurriedly resolved to send for Amarault, tell him all was forgotten and forgiven, and thus disarm him of at least one incentive to harm Arasilus. She had already discovered enough of Amarault's real character to believe that he would stop at no means whereby to gain his ends, and knowing as she did the story of his mother's character, even to the foul means she resorted to with the priest to wrong Arasilus, and place her own son in the royal seat, she felt that he inherited the vileness which he now displayed.

Yet, despite of the loathing that she felt at meeting again with one so vile, one who had wronged and insulted her so deeply, still for her dear lord's sake, she would count her own feelings as naught, and humble herself for his safety. Exercised by these considerations, she sent word to Amarault that she would see him at his convenience, indeed that she hoped he would come to her at once in her private closet, and with this desire expressed on paper, she sent him the note by an attendant, receiving an answer by the return of Amarault himself. He came flushed with wine, and exalted at the idea of being thus summoned by her who had but the day before so rudely and proudly repulsed him from her presence.

Esmah suppressed the disgust she felt, and only sought to appease the anger of Amarault. She told him that perhaps she herself was more to blame than he, that her manner or her speech perhaps was not sufficiently guarded; in short, that she had been thinking most seriously of the difference between them, and wished once more to become friends with him. She assured him that she should forget that which had passed, so that he continued her husband's good friend, nor should Arasilus ever know that there had any misunderstanding existed between them. In her generous spirit, and her anxiety for her absent lord, she humbled herself before the heartless and revengeful cousin of the king, and begged his forgiveness, though in fact she had committed no fault to be forgiven.

But she mistook the man, after all, in appealing to his generosity; it was a quality, which, if he possessed at all, had lain so long inactive in his heart, as to have become dormant forever. He listened to her with a bitter smile, he looked upon her wondrous beauty with increased passion, and all heated as he was with the fumes of the wine, he could only comprehend that Esmah, in all her unequalled beauty, was before him, and a suppliant.

"Lady," said he, "I have gone too far, have already risked too much to turn back unrequited; either give me thy favor, or I will have such revenge as neither you nor your husband dream of—you shall both be crushed in the fulfilment of my promise."

"Think not I fear thee for myself, but alas! I would my lord were here and safe," Esmah almost sobbed, "here to punish thee for thy perfidy."

The spirit of evil was burning in Amarault's breast; he approached the queen and said, "Come, lady, it is a fitting hour for love, and we are alone."

Esmah shrank back, trembling and dismayed at his look.

"Nay, think not to escape me," he said, turning and fastening the door. "We are in a wing of the palace, far away from those who would answer thy call, and thou thyself hast taken care to send away thy waiting-maids. Come, I say, you have not sent for me without a purpose."

"My lord, my lord, O, for the love of Heaven, approach me not!"

"Nay, lady, I am in earnest, be assured," replied Amarault, seizing the queen by the arm, and drawing her towards him with rudeness.

A slight shriek burst from Esmah as he seized her, but his hand upon her mouth suppressed it, so that it could scarcely be heard beyond her own door. But scarce a moment had transpired after that faint cry was uttered, when the rich tapestry that curtained the room was lifted, and a figure leaped through a secret door in the wainscotting. Amarault started back in wonder as he saw the muzzle of a long Turkish pistol pointed at his head, held in the steady though long and bony hands of the dwarf.

Esmah, profiting by the astonishment that possessed Amarault,

sprang away from him, and sinking upon the floor behind the
dwarf, sobbed as though her heart would break. How strange
the picture of that beautiful being, almost angelic in loveliness.
guarded by so hideous a form that the eye almost ached to look
upon it. Yet, though thus misshapen, the dwarf looked almost
handsome now. One arm and hand were held before the prostrate Esmah, while with the other his weapon was held pointed
at the villain who had attacked a defenceless woman. The eye
of the dwarf, to which we have more than once referred, presented a strange appearance now; its soft, tender, woman-like
beauty had vanished, and there seemed to pour from it such a
flash of rage and resolution, that Amarault was satisfied that
his life hung upon a thread, and that were he to advance one
step towards the queen, a bullet would pierce his brain.

Almost crazed with rage, he bit his lips until the very blood
started from them, and walking towards the door, turned with
a meaning glance to the dwarf, and with an oath to himself, he
burst away from the scene.

When he was gone, the dwarf replaced the weapon within
his bosom, and in an instant his whole manner was changed.
He was once more the simple, docile, forsaken-looking creature,
who had followed the princess from her father's harem to
Greece; his eyes once more beamed softly and happily upon
his mistress, and placing himself near the door whence Amarault
had departed, he coiled himself in a corner, and was as inani-
mate, in appearance, as though life was no longer in him.
Esmah could only look her gratitude to the poor dumb creature,
and taking his big cold hand within her own delicate one, she
pressed it to her heart with tears upon her cheek. A deep
guttural sound, the only one the dwarf ever made, signified his
appreciation of her gratitude. But when she had returned
within the inner apartment of her chamber to seek the rest her
nerves so much required, the dwarf laid the hand she had held
against his own rude breast, and tears filled his eyes. Heaven
only could know his inward thoughts!

Baffled in his plans, Amarault grew more resolved upon the
ruin of Esmah, and he knew that if he could accomplish that,
Arasilus, who held her as the apple of his eye, the very core of
his heart, would also fall before the shock. He knew that if he
could ruin the domestic bliss of the king, that he would at once
retire from the court, such was his delicate nature, and, of
course, his own right to the throne of Greece would then be

undisputed. In pursuance of this heartless and villanous purpose, he found it necessary to employ a trusty and unscrupulous
agent; and such a one fortune had formed to his hand, in a
young and dissipated hanger-on at the court.

Cassimir was a young Greek of some eight and twenty years,
whose life had passed away in luxuriant indolence, he being
the only son of a rich and noble house at Athens. Profligate
in his nature, and a constant gambler, and improvident to the
last degree, he had now quite exhausted the ample means he
had inherited, and was often indebted to Amarault for small
pecuniary loans, wherewith to keep up the appearance of a
gentleman at court. The king's cousin had marked him well,
and had long since adopted him only because he felt that he
would stop at no deed, however vile, if he could only realize
gold by its commission. The position which Amarault had for
some time found himself in, told him that the time would one
day come when such a person, reckless, willing, and resolute,
might be of eminent service to him, and therefore it was that he
befriended Cassimir, supplying him with means to satisfy his
vitiated appetite for gaming and luxury.

Through this agent Amarault was determined to lay a plan
to blast the fair fame of Esmah, and to prove so foul a stain
upon her name, that even Arasilus himself would refuse ever
again to behold her. With this resolution he sought the presence of his poor, deluded, half-ruined tool, and over a bottle of
wine prepared him for the part he was to perform.

" Cassimir, it is a high game we are to play, and we have no
common persons to deal with. The lady is strong in virtue and
honor; these are the barriers we are to attack—not by quietly
laying siege to them and starving them out, but by a bold *coup
de main* carry the citadel at once. Her husband is no trifler,
and nothing short of the strongest confirmation will affect him,
and even this must be carefully arranged, lest by reason of his
shrewdness, it might fail."

"But who are the parties, my good lord? you name them
not."

" Of that, more anon. A goblet of this wine to thee, Cassimir.
I pledge you to the success of our enterprise, which, if successful, shall be a thousand ounces of gold in thy purse."

"A thousand ounces? that is a goodly sum indeed," replied
the spendthrift.

" The price of thy fidelity in this business," replied the other.

" Well, now for the parties; who are they?" asked Cassimir again.

" Fill again; this is the best of Persian vintage," said Amarault, who wished to prime his victim well with courage ere he revealed on whom he was to work.

" Right, it is good wine," replied Cassimir, tossing off another glass. " But who did you say were the characters in this farce?"

" It is the wife of my cousin, Arasilus, the king," said Amarault.

" The queen!" whispered Cassimir, half dropping the glass he held, while he gazed at Amarault with a flushed cheek and bloodshot eyes.

" Ay, the queen," replied Amarault, with assumed indifference. " She is mortal, the same as you or I. Come, more wine."

" I have no taste for more," replied the other, pushing the glass from him.

" Nay, you do not show the white feather, Cassimir, with such a purse within thy grasp as a thousand ounces of gold!" said the tempter, jokingly.

" I would it were some other business, my lord, that you required of me; for truth to say, I much respect our noble queen, and Arasilus himself, who is every inch a king. But as you say, this is glorious wine, my lord. I pledge you again," said the already heated youth.

Amarault understood his man, and a few more glasses raised his courage and recklessness to the necessary point for his purpose. This once accomplished, Amarault was satisfied, for he knew that he would keep the promises which he elicited from him as to the business.

CHAPTER XVI.

THE PLOT AGAINST THE HONOR OF ESMAH.

HAVING ensured to himself the services of the profligate Cassimír, Amarault now resolved at once to set about the ruin of his cousin's domestic peace, by blasting the character of his queen. By shrewd, half-defined hints from himself and Cassimír, the court was prepared for the coming event by their suspicion being roused, without their really knowing why or how, and already curious eyes were directed towards the wife of Arasilus when she moved abroad. All went on as the artful Amarault desired. The queen was an object of suspicion, and now it rested with him, by some single event of a decisive character, to produce some combination of circumstances that should so fix guilt upon her that no one could possibly doubt her unfaithfulness.

Amarault so contrived as to induce a half dozen of his court to rise with the sun one morning, to join him in an equestrian excursion without the precincts of the city. They were to rendezvous in the grand hall of the palace at the earliest dawn, and, passing out together, mount and away. The morning came, and with it the courtiers assembled to meet Amarault, and booted and spurred they all passed along the corridor together, towards the court-yard below. The passage led them by the private entrance to the queen's suite of chambers, and the moment they came in sight of the door, a cavalier, wrapped in a cloak, sprang from it, as though he came from the queen's chamber, and rushed away.

With a burst of well-affected astonishment, Amarault pretended to pursue the stranger sword in hand, but he soon escaped in the labyrinth of passages, and returning to the grand hall, Amarault said:

"Friends, the startling evidence of the guilt of the queen which we have all witnessed, so unmans me that I cannot ride to-day. I pray for the credit of the king, for your love to me and the honor of the throne, that you will be silent concerning this which you have seen."

"This but substantiates," said one, "the whispers that have been uttered about the court for some days relative to the queen."

"Did you recognize the individual, my lord?" asked another, of Amarault.

"I should know him, if we met again," he replied; "though I was not able to overtake him at the moment, in the darkness of the corridor."

"He was tall in person," said another; "about the height of Cassimir, I should say."

At this moment Cassimir entered from the grand reception hall, in a direction which he could only have reached from without the palace, unless, indeed, he had passed through the private apartments of Amarault, which, of course, were not accessible to any one. If a suspicion of him had crossed the courtier's mind who had named him, as of about the height of the stranger, it was dispelled at once by his appearance so immediately in the dress he usually wore, from another direction, and in the most calm and unruffled spirits, evincing, at the story he had heard, the most unbounded surprise, and declaring that he wished he had been present at the time.

"Friends, I may require your advice in this matter ere long," said Amarault; "but at present my feelings are such that I would seek the quiet of my closet. Alas! that so foul a stain should have come upon the honor of our king. Friends, I beg you excuse me."

"My lord, your feelings are most natural," said the eldest of the courtiers.

Then turning to the rest, he observed:

"Friends, with our fingers on our lips, let us take leave of the prince, and, with goodly caution, keep within our own breasts that which we have seen."

"We are holden to do so," they answered, in one voice.

Thus saying, the party separated, not in good faith to keep their own counsel, as had been suggested, but secretly each one to impart the suspicions that had been aroused to some intimate friend, who, in turn, would divulge it to another, and from him it would become public property, and thus the innocence of the queen was subjected to the vilest suspicions. Though this was against the expressed wish of Amarault, yet it was in exact accordance with his desires, and his agent, Cassimir, reported the progress of the scandal to him that very night, while both sipped their wine together in the private room of the king's cousin. Villany, sad villany, was at work against poor Esmah.

On the subsequent day, Amarault, having prepared the following paper, obtained the signatures of those who witnessed his plot, with the purpose of transmitting it at once to the king, who was at Constantinople on important business of state.

The paper was artfully worded, so as to commit those who signed it, and read as follows:

"We, good and loyal subjects of King Arasilus of Greece, with sorrowful hearts do herein express our grief at what we have seen, and what we are constrained to bear testimony to. To wit, that the wife of our lord, the queen of Greece, has proved, in the absence of her noble spouse, unfaithful to her vows. At first we heard, but believed not, the reports that were on every tongue concerning the queen's disloyalty, until constrained by our own eyes, which bore us unwilling witness of her frailty and dishonor, to believe that the king is foully wronged by his wife. This sad evidence we bear, and solicit of your royal highness that you do at once return to heal your wounded honor."

With so strong a document as this, signed by six of the best names at court, the crafty Amarault felt that he could easily accomplish his object. In soliciting their names to the paper which he had drawn up, he did so with such well-affected sorrow that they scarcely read what they signed, and much less weighed its branding import, literally signing away a pure lady's honor as lightly as they would have witnessed a simple state document.

It was late that night, on which the paper was signed, that Amarault visited the queen. It was the first time he had seen her since the interference of the dwarf. He came to her with a malignant smile, and coolly told her what had been witnessed by these courtiers, and read to her the paper that they had unitedly signed, to be sent by express to her husband. He watched her every expression to see the effect upon her, but instead of the trembling frame and agitation that he looked for, he read the proud defiance of her heart baptized in purity and honor, and he even quailed before the clear, piercing look that she bent upon him, as though she would read his very soul. He had thought her a woman as weak as she was beautiful, one on whom he could work his wiles with sure success, but he found that the armor of virtue was impervious to his rude and unholy attack, and he felt like the knight who, in his headlong career against his antagonist, shivers his lance, and is himself unhorsed. At last, as both sat there in silence, the queen thus far not having spoken one word, she asked, while she still gazed intently upon Amarault, watching the workings of his heart in his face:

"And, under these circumstances, what do you counsel me to do?"

"Your safest course is instant flight to your father at Constantinople."

"Would it be the part of *innocence* to fly my husband's palace?"

"I have nothing to do with innocence or guilt. I speak of the position of affairs," said Amarault. "By flying at once you will reach your father immediately after Arasilus leaves him, as I shall send a courier at once from here to carry these tidings and papers to the king."

"You do not await his return, then?" asked the queen.

"To-morrow morning sees a small escort, with Cassimir at its head, on the road to the East."

"This irrevocably fixed upon?" asked the queen, with much interest.

"It is, lady, unless you please to revoke it yourself," said Amarault, struggling between his passion and ambition, as he gazed upon the loveliness before him.

"Can I revoke it, then?" asked the queen, quickly.

"Grant me your favor, and the whole suspicion and charge shall be annulled, and your innocence shall be made as clear as the light of day."

"So to prove my innocence you would have me become guilty!" said the queen, with a scornful expression of irony playing about her handsome lips.

"It is the only course left," replied the villain, quietly.

"Then let me tell thee," said the queen, rising in dignity as she spoke, and drawing a bright dagger from her belt, "that sooner than listen to thy vile proposals, this steel shall drink my heart's blood. I fear thee not, thou villain; send to my noble lord whatever thou wilt, he will not believe thee; and, when he does return, woe to them who have thus striven to betray his honor and mine. Send to my lord, tell what, thou wilt, and he will beard it with the lie. We have loved too well, have been too long together, have proved each other's love too thoroughly, my lord, not to know the honesty of our hearts, and their truthfulness to each other."

" We will soon see, as to that, my confident one. Your husband has been accustomed to trust such names as are attached to this paper, and will not consider their evidence lightly," said Amarault, as he retired to meet Cassimir, and instruct him for the mission that would start on the morrow for the East.

On the following morning the young courtier, Cassimir, accompanied by some dozen attendants in various capacities, more, however, to give him that dignity and consideration which was so agreeable to his vanity, than for any actual service they might render, started for the coast, from whence they were to take a vessel, and, doubling the southern coast of Negropont, stand up the Ægean Sea through the Dardanelles and the Sea of Marmora to Constantinople. He had received ample instructions from his employer as to the part he was to perform, and went doubly primed with the importance of his mission and the recollection of the gold he was to receive for the part he played in this plot to ruin the queen's reputation.

After reaching the coast, the party embarked for their port of destination; but, as they were all unused to the sea, they were at once seized with that nauseating and woe-begone malady, called sea-sickness. We say all, but there was a single exception, a priest, who was attached to the court, and, indeed, who had acted as confessor to the royal family. He had been detailed by Amarault, at the request of the vain-glorious Cassimir, to accompany him to the sultan's court. The priest was unmoved by the motion of the small vessel in which they embarked, as it regarded any sickness, and was found ever ready to assist his comrades.

But at last they bore up towards the north; after doubling Cape Negropont, one of the fiercer squalls set in that blow so furiously in these inland seas, and the little bark struggled as though her fate were sealed. Even her captain, a stern, weather-beaten sailor, who had coasted in the Ægean Sea for half his life, looked troubled; and, to the many and frequent inquiries addressed to him by the party, acknowledged that death was staring them full in the face, and that unless the squall, which had now ripened into a fierce Levanter, should lull, they must, most assuredly, all go down together.

At this juncture Cassimir, pale and trembling, presenting a most vivid picture of fear and physical debility, besought the priest to shrive him ere it should be too late.

"Would you confess at this hour, my son?" asked the priest.

"Ay, father, and quickly, for there are but a few moments left us at best."

"Then follow me to the cabin," said the priest, leading the way.

Here, in a corner of the apartment, the proud, unprincipled profligate knelt to the priest, who breathed a short but pertinent prayer, and then turning to Cassimir bade him in brief and in truth to confess his sins before God, who alone had power to pardon and forgive. "I, as his humble instrument, will listen to you," said the priest, laying his cross upon his lap. It was then that Cassimir, after glancing at a life of profligacy and sin, came to the last act in which he was now engaged, to blast the fair name of an innocent woman. He confessed that it was himself who had contrived to be near the queen's door at the moment in the morning when the party passed there, and that he had rushed away to give the appearance of having left her sleeping room, as well as that it was he who had originated every story against her, for all of which he was to be richly paid by Amarault, had not this fatality overreached them.

The priest heard the story to the end, gently chided the sinner, but told him if he repented the acts he had done, that he, as the humble instrument only, forgave him, and then recommended him to devote the few moments left of life to sincere prayer to Heaven. And then he went with kind assurance to one and another of the afflicted and bewildered passengers, who, even in their terror, paused to wonder at his calmness at such a trying moment.

Promises and resolutions made in storms, says the proverb, are forgotten in calms; and thus it was with Cassimir. As the gale gradually subsided, and the little bark rode once more in comparative safety upon the bosom of the sea, he felt all his worldly ties and attractions once more asserting their power in his heart, and he began to charge himself with unmanly fear, and of needlessly betraying his own secret to the priest, although he had no fear on that account, for full well he knew the sacredness of the confessional, and that aught thus divulged was as sacred in the keeping of the priest as though it had never been uttered. At least that was the way he had been educated to believe, and he had never seen reason to doubt its correctness.

It will not, therefore, be wondered at that he renewed his arrangements and looked forward with confidence to the accomplishment of his original object in the voyage, as it regarded representations that he was to make and sustain before Arasilus. And thus they all sped on up the Marmora and Bosphorus to the fair bay whose waters lave the shores of Constantinople.

Some two days subsequent to the departure of Cassimir and his party, Amarault found, to his no small delight, that the queen had left the palace, no one knew how, and gone, no one knew where. ".Is it possible," he thought, "that she has adopted my advice, after all, and has gone to her husband? Doubtless this is the case; but, unless I can anticipate her arrival at the court of the sultan, this flight will be of no avail to me," reasoned the cunning Amarault. "It must be made to appear that, when her guilt was discovered, she escaped from the palace, perhaps with the object of her guilt, but, at any rate, being discovered, she fled."

Reasoning thus, Amarault summoned the best courier to be found in Athens, and, with private instructions which he wrote out for Cassimir, promised the man most princely pay provided he would reach Constantinople before the vessel in which the party already referred to had sailed, and liberally supplying the courier with means, he sent him off at once.

But for the storm which Cassimir and his party encountered, the courier's mission would have been fruitless. But as it was, he first arrived at the city of Mahomet, and there awaited the coming of Cassimir, to whom he delivered his despatches. Of course, with this additional item of seeming-guilt, he would be able to make out a far stronger case than he would else have done, and he blessed his stars, in the vileness of his heart, that the queen had fled from the court, even though she was coming hither, for he did not doubt that Arasilus would instantly start for home, and the possibility of their meeting would be frustrated; for the lady would doubtless travel slowly, and could scarcely by any possible chance, take such a route as should lead her to meet her lord on the way.

So certain of success was Cassimir now, that he did not even detain the courier until he should hold an interview with Aras-

ilus, but despatched him back again straight with flattering
promises to his employer. The courier was riding for gold,
and back he went to claim the reward of his hardly accomplished
purpose.

To another chapter we must refer the reader for the meeting
between the king Arasilus, and he who brought such foul
tidings from the court of Athens.

CHAPTER XVII.

THE FAITHLESS COURTIER BEFORE HIS KING.

No sooner was Cassimir announced at the quarters of the
Greek king Arasilus, in Constantinople, than he was admitted
with his suite, consisting of the priest and his immediate attendant, who acted as secretary. Arasilus received them graciously,
and honorably welcomed them in the most generous impulse of
his heart, and asked in the same breath after the health and
well-being of his honored and dearly-loved wife. But he
observed some singular emotion move them as he spoke of her,
and so he asked again more hurriedly and earnestly than before.
But still the eyes of the three were averted, and they seemed
loth to speak of her at all. Alarmed at this, Arasilus, almost
trembling at the idea, feared some bodily ill had befallen her.

"Speak, for the love of Heaven! Tell me my wife is well, that
no ill has happened to her, and I will bless you all."

"We left her well in *body*, my lord," said Cassimir, significantly.

"O, I thank you for that," replied Arasilus, too much over-
joyed at the answer to note the hidden sarcasm; "for if aught
were to befall her, life were worthless to us. But, gentlemen,
what brings you to Constantinople? Some business of state, I
should suspect, some matter of more than ordinary importance,
or else you would hardly have come this long and tedious way."

"Business, my lord," said Cassimir, "of such grave import
that our tongues cleave to our mouths when we strive to utter
it."

"Nay, speak out," said Arasilus, calmly; "so our queen be

well, we care not for the freak that fortune may have played us
Have the provinces revolted? Has some one mounted the
throne in my absence? Come, speak out, gentlemen."

"Nay, my lord, none of these," replied Cassimir, "but it is of
the queen we would speak."

"The queen!" said Arasilus, again starting to his feet. "You
just told me, sir, that you left her well at Athens. What mean
you? Speak no more in riddles, unless you wish to incur our
fixed displeasure, but at once to the business that has brought
you here."

"Well, then, my lord, though loth I am to tell it, I will at
once proceed in the unwelcome task that has brought me to
you. So, please you, my lord, this letter is from your cousin,
and these papers are for your perusal with it."

Arasilus seized the papers eagerly, and with a quick eye ran
them over, while the expression of his face, in the meantime,
evinced the passion that raged in his breast, and the storm of
his temper that was gathering so quickly. He asked one more
hurried question, but his voice, when next he spoke, was slow,
but so deep and calm that even the priest seemed to start at its
tones. His comprehensive mind had at once taken in the whole
idea of the papers. He saw the import in a moment, and turning to Cassimir, he asked:

"What is the meaning of all this, my lord? Why do you
bring such stuff to me?"

"Stuff?"

"Ay, that's my word," said the king, meaningly.

"Stuff, my lord?" said Cassimir, confidently. "It is proof,
unmistakable proof."

"Of what?" asked the king, bending his piercing eye upon
the speaker.

"The queen's *disloyalty*, my lord, and your dishonor."

"Ha!" said the king, seizing Cassimir by the throat, "unsay
that word—unsay it quickly, or by this light you die!"

"My lord, my lord, if I would, I could not. This very hour
I have received intelligence from your cousin that she has fled
from Athens, and all the court know her guilty."

The king's rapier glanced from its scabbard, as though spon-
taneously and of its own accord, and the next moment it had
pierced the heart of the foul being who had thus belied the
character of the queen.

"Thus perish all who say as much as a breath to tarnish the

fair fame of one who is next to the angels in purity and truth
and as far above the reach of such poor malice as thine, my
cousin's, and all his backers, as the stars are above our heads.

"He said she has fled from the court. He would hardly have
said *that*, unless it was true," mused the king. "What could
have taken her from home? May be persecution—may be she
fled to escape her tormentors. By the heaven above us, let her
motive have been what it may, still she is pure and true to me!
Give me but room to swing this right arm, and place me among
them, and I will write the lie on the front of the boldest of them.
A goodly business, truly, to attack the honor of the queen in
her lord's absence—a noble employment for the court at Athens.
I had thought better of even Amarault than this—though, of
a truth, he has lately given me some strange tokens of his
duplicity. Attack the honor of the queen! By the crown we
wear, it shall go heavy with these slanderers; they shall be
made to swear that she is as pure as the light, and as scathless
as virtue itself."

Thus he mused, half to himself and half aloud, for some
moments, chafing at the anger that filled his breast—the honest
indignation that filled his heart at the insult his queen and himself had sustained in this business.

His passion had passed away with the surfeit his vengeance
had wreaked upon the now lifeless body before him, and order-
ing it removed, he bade the secretary and priest to hasten back
to Athens, whence he should soon follow them, and look after
the knaves and fools who had been playing so deep a game in
his absence from the throne.

"I am more surprised to see you here, reverend father," said
the king, "on such a mission as this, lending by your presence
an aspect of piety to the damning lie that foul carcase uttered.
You were better employed, believe us, in holy offices at home,
nor could I have thought that you, who knew the queen so
well, for all that is pure and good, could for a moment consent
to rest supinely, while this unrighteous business has been ripe-
ning. We feel grieved at this, holy father."

"So please you, my lord, permit the clerk to retire, and
grant me a moment of private audience," said the priest, from
beneath his ghostly cowl.

"Retire," said the king to the secretary; "and, stay—make
all haste, thou and thy people, to embark again quickly for
Athens. I shall return by land."

The humble secretary, trembling in every limb at the summary justice that he had seen administered to his late master, was only too happy to leave the king's presence, and hasted away to the vessel, where he told as much of his story as he dared, and bade them prepare again for sea.

Scarcely had the door closed upon the person of the clerk, when the cowl and cloak dropped from the supposed priest, and discovered the person of the queen!

"Is this a miracle?" exclaimed Arasilus, starting back and gazing with undisguised astonishment at the sight before him.

"No miracle but thine own Esmah," said the queen, bursting into a flood of tears upon his neck.

"How came you here with these vilifiers?" asked the king.

"You shall hear," said the queen, through her tears of joy.

"Nay, dearest, think not that they have ruffled me much."

"I knew you would not believe the vile story, my kind lord," said the queen, clinging fondly to the king's neck.

"Not for one moment, my wife, not a breath of such slander."

Esmah could only cling still closer to his heart in her happiness.

"Come, dearest, sit thee here and explain all this foul business to me."

"I will, I will, cheerfully, my dear, dear husband."

"But first wipe away those tears," said the king, affectionately, as he drew her to his side, and listened to her story.

After a little regaining her self-possession, she told Arasilus of the foul plot that had been laid to destroy her fair name, and that she was so much astonished at the well-connived arrangements of the design, that she determined to come herself to Constantinople in disguise, to look after her honor, and see how such news would be received by her husband. As it would make but a few moments' delay in the ultimate discovery, she let the plot go on undisturbed, until she saw the noble estimate that the king placed upon her, and how little he heeded the black falsehood that was told him against her, whom he trusted and believed in all this. She told him of her disguise, and how she had managed to deceive all, even Cassimir himself, who, in his fright, confessed his crime to her, which he had now expiated with his life. She told him of the scene, too, where the dwarf had so befriended her at a critical moment, and finally how she had by entreaty prevailed upon the good father confessor to permit her to don his attire, and thus escape from the court. The priest himself had never for a moment heeded the reports that were circulated, and thinking that it was perhaps for the best, acceded to the queen's desire, and aided her all in his power.

Arasilus was now all impatience to settle his business with the sultan, and to return to chastise his crafty cousin, and to see the honesty of his wife's integrity once more fully established at Athens. But Esmah was now in the city of her nativity, and within a few moments' walk of her father's palace, her proud old father, who had ever been so kind and affectionate to her, and whom in turn she loved so fondly. She must see him; some plausible excuse must be made for her sudden appearance at Constantinople, and then she would return again with her husband. It was resolved that a happy surprise should be managed, to delight and astonish the sultan, and this Arasilus and Esmah arranged together, and the subsequent day, after Esmah had assumed the dress that became her sex and station, the old sultan was astonished by seeing his daughter walk into his private apartments and throw herself fondly by his side and upon his breast.

"God is great," said the sultan, wiping a tear from either eye, while he pressed his favorite and long-absent child to his heart.

For good reasons it was thought best between Esmah and Arasilus that his identity as the page should never be made known to the sultan, though the fact of the ambassador and the king being one and the same had already transpired; indeed, it was known as soon as he re-appeared at Constantinople upon the summons of the sultan. Sometimes the feelings of the page would come over him, and he yearned to tell the proud old Turk that the boy whom he had treated so kindly, was now the king who stood as an equal before him. But there were reasons that we need not refer to here, but which are obvious, that rendered secrecy on this point the best policy, and therefore both himself and Esmah observed the most profound silence upon the subject. The lapse of years, the change of style and bearing, the effect of rank, and above all, the well-authenticated death of the page, put all suspicion as to the fact referred to, entirely at rest, and therefore he had no fear of discovery in any contingency, unless favored by himself.

With what delight did Esmah and himself roam over those well-remembered paths in the seraglio gardens, recalling every incident of their childish days together, and now without fear of intrusion enjoying the many delightful belongings of the place. How long they sat together in that well-remembered spot marked by the bent cypress, and told over anew their stories, and vowed again each their loves.

"What a contrast is presented, Esmah," he would say, "between this hour and those that we passed here, first as children, then as lovers, and now as king and queen of Athens!"

"The title, dear Arasilus, I heed not, but your ever constant love and truth are all in all to me, and sometimes I think that I am only too happy, for everything goes well with us. Even this apparent misfortune that had seemed to beset me in thy absence, has terminated in renewed joys and pleasure—my unanticipated visit here yielding unlooked-for joy to us both."

"It is all the recompense of true love, Esmah," he smilingly replied.

The business that had brought him to Constantinople was now soon terminated, and with his happy wife by his side, he turned his face towards Athens. The way was long, but they pursued it industriously and without hindrance for many days, until they reached the city, even before the party who had started by water, and thus Arasilus brought back the first news of Cassimir's punishment and death for promulgating the black falsehood started by his cousin.

The smooth-faced villany of Amarault, his profuse offers of proof, and his unblushing charge against the queen, were all met by Arasilus with a prompt order for his arrest, and a proclamation for his early trial before the court. Then it was that the true character of the weak-minded Amarault showed itself. He broke down completely under the resolute treatment of his cousin, the king, scarcely made an effort for his defence before the court, and finally, after the trial, frankly acknowledged his guilt, though not until he was condemned to the scaffold.

It was a mild, serene night in the Grecian capital. The moon tipped alike the lofty pillars of the temples and the frowning angles of the prison walls, when a figure, wrapped in a long and heavy cloak, presented itself at the prison gate, and showing a signet upon its hand, passed each wary sentinel even to the inner keep. The profound respect that was shown this personage evinced at once the rank that must belong to the wearer of the signet, and the captain of the prison opened the door and disappeared with the visitor, lighting the way along the deep and dreary halls.

They entered the apartment devoted to the prince Amarault, and there found the miserable, weak-minded man leaning upon a rude table, and manacled. He looked up vacantly as they entered, with despair written in every lineament of his haggard features.

"Strike off those irons," said a voice that came from female lips, and at the words of which Amarault started and almost trembled.

The prisoner gazed with dumb astonishment upon them both.

The keeper obeyed the order, and in a moment after the prisoner's limbs were released.

"Amarault," said the queen, for it was she, "you were most cruel and unkind to me, and at a moment when I had a right to look to you for protection; but had you known me better, I think you had not used me thus. To show you that I bear you who now confess and profess repentance, no malice, I have begged of my noble lord for your pardon. Here it is; and now Amarault, you are free, with the simple proviso that you are banished from Athens."

"Heaven bless you, my royal lady," said the broken hearted man, falling at her feet. "O, had I learned to love your sex truly and honorably, had I chosen to myself a companion who would have made me honor her sex as thou dost influence me now, it had been different with me, lady. Alas! I sometimes fear that I have inherited somewhat of my unfortunate character, and then I hope that I may be more freely forgiven, lady. Your forgiveness is sweet to me now, sweeter even than freedom, for life has few charms for me. I shall go far away, but shall never forget to pray, hourly and truly, for heaven's choicest blessings on you and yours!"

Amarault left those prison walls an altered man, humbled and reformed. Kindness had done that which no force or law could have accomplished; the active kindness of her whom he would have so foully wronged, completed his reformation. With an earnest farewell, he left the prison, alone, unattended, and without seeing the countenance of a human being, he passed out of the city to find a home among strangers.

The fair fame of the queen was as pure and unsullied as the stars, and she was scarcely less honored and beloved than the people's favorite himself, King Arasilus.

CHAPTER XVIII.

THE RECLUSE OF THE MOUNTAINS.

AT nightfall, some years subsequent to the close of the last chapter, a small troop of horse, well attended and sumptuously found, were filing through the far-famed pass of Thermopylæ. The setting sun threw a powerful light upon the broken monument of the brave Leonidas, who offered up his life on this spot, with his brother soldiers, in behalf of Greece, and in opposition to the almost numberless host of Persians led by Xerxes and his generals. The troop might have numbered two score, including servants, pages, and men-at-arms. At the head rode a lady and knight, with those unmistakable tokens about them that stamped them at once as nobles, and more than that, of royal blood.

It was Arasilus and his queen, who had been here examining together the pass that forms the entrance to Greece from the northeast, and which the annals of history have rendered so famous. They were unchanged, save a more matured manliness sat upon the king's brow, and time had only served to ripen the passing loveliness of the queen, while her glance of pride and love ever and anon at her lord, told how truly dear he still was to her; nor would you have to gaze long to see that his every word and action showed how tenderly and dearly he considered her by his side.

As they entered within the opening grounds from the pass to the south, they passed abruptly the pointed and angular base of the mountain, coming suddenly upon the person of one whose dress and manner bespoke him to be a recluse. The king reined up and spoke him fair, offering a purse for his necessities, but the humble man bowed low and told the monarch that he needed it not.

" What brings you to these mountain passes, and why do you

live here, excluded from all human beings?" asked the king, kindly.

The hermit approached him more close, and said, in a low voice:

"For repentance and to seek forgiveness of Heaven for my sins. It is years since I slept beneath a roof, and long and severe is the penance I have done; but I am happy now. I feel that I am forgiven. Do you not know me?"

"Indeed, no," said the king, with much interest, "I know you not."

"I am thy cousin Amarault. Farewell, farewell!" And as he spoke he disappeared within the tangled foliage of the mountain, while the troop moved on.

Desiring further audience of his unhappy cousin, the king, dismounting, sought to follow him, but soon lost his track in the intricate woods, and returning to his steed, mounted again, resolving at a more fitting time to return and seek out the repentant one, and endeavor to restore him to the comforts of life, if not to his former position. But as we shall follow him no further, it is perhaps best for us to close his story here, and say, that although the king and his servants were never able to find him afterwards, yet it was not many years subsequent, that a shepherd discovered a skeleton upon one of the upper ridges of the mountain, its bones bleached by the action of the storm and sunshine, and these were gathered and had honorable burial at Athens, as the remains of the evil-minded but repentant Amarault.

But to return to the king and his fair company in the pass. The froth upon the bridles of the troop, and the smoking flanks of the horses, showed that they had been long in the saddle, and they spurred on to the nearest hostelry for refreshment and rest.

In this part of our story we must not forget to speak of the dwarf—the silent, vigilant, affectionate attendant that has so often appeared in these scenes. Of all the court at Athens, none were more happy, none more contented than this poor, deformed, faithful creature. His apartments in the palace were furnished with every comfort and even luxury that could be procured; the rooms were in the most private part of the palace, and adjoining those of the king and queen. Every consideration was had for his comfort and happiness; and childlike and happy he sped on his humble way to the end of life, enjoying its smiles much more than many another who seemed far better calculated by fortune to do so. His important services, first in aiding the king, when he was a humble page at the Turkish palace in the seraglio, when the bloodthirsty Turk had him in his grasp, and his second, and, if possible, still more valued aid at the fearful moment when the queen, alone and unprotected, was attacked by Amarault, were not forgotten; and to evince the gratitude that he felt to his dumb and simple friend, Arasilus had a golden medal engraved, bearing upon one side the fallen Turk, himself and the dwarf, and on the reverse the scene, where with extended weapon and standing before the queen, the dwarf had threatened the villain who would have seized her. The dwarf could fully appreciate such a token, and he valued it most highly, never being seen without the golden record about his neck.

In that part of the palace devoted to the accommodation of the immediate officers of the royal household, sat a lady, toying with a fair-haired child. You would have paused with delight to see that young mother and her infant, both so pure, so lovely and so innocent. The child crowed and laughed with ecstatic glee, and the mother's heart leaped for joy at the happy spirit of her infant. If you had heeded her well, she would have recalled to your mind a familiar face, and a link in the story we have told you. And now there enters one whose manly figure and fine, good-natured face, expressive of intelligence and good humor, seem the only requisites necessary to complete this picture of domestic happiness. He, too, the reader might have recognized by a little observation, as he tossed the child playfully in the air, and then kissed both its little lips, and afterwards those of the mother. Ah, they were very happy. It was evident in every look, in every word.

" Our dear boy grows prettier every day," said he who held the child.

"And more and more like you," said the happy wife.

"Are we thankful enough, dearest, for this pure little spirit that God hath given us to rear and love?" asked the father, gazing with pride upon his child.

" Daily, nightly, hourly is my voice lifted up for him," said the mother.

" I have good news for you, wife, good news, that will please you."

" Indeed, and what is it?"

"Your father comes to-day. I have this morning heard from Negropont."

"Ah, my dear, good father. And I will return with him for a few days."

"As you will. It will gratify your kind mother, dearest."

"Will you not go too? You will, I am sure."

"If you wish it, yes," said the husband, kindly.

It was the gentle, kind-hearted Nydia and her husband, Alazar, that formed this picture. Grateful for the hospitality he had experienced at her father's humble cot on the island of Negropont, and knowing full well that from this class he could draw the safest in his endeavors to surround himself with honest and trusty officers, the king had, soon after having discovered himself to them, as we have already described, called Alazar to court and appointed him to a trusty and lucrative post in his household, where, with his wife, he had lived· happily several years, the queen herself befriending Nydia, and telling her that she should ever love her for the disinterested kindness she had shown to the king, when he was a humble and shipwrecked slave.

Esmah made not one only, but many visits to the sultan, her father. The good old Mahometan was affectionate to her, and loaded his favorite child with the most costly presents that his wealth and power could procure. He was still proud of her, and when she came, the city was illuminated, and regal honors waited upon her.

"Father," said Esmah, the last time she visited the seraglio, "I have one thing which I would fain tell to thee, if you will promise not to be displeased."

"O, you cannot displease me, my dear child," said the sultan.

"Then, father, you remember the page Alick, who served you so well, and whom you loved so well, too, but who for some reason fled with the royal yacht from your service?"

"The boy was a Greek, and saved thy life in the Bosphorus?" said the sultan.

"Yes, father, the same," said Esmah, pleased to see his vivid recollection, for he was getting old and infirm now, and sinking apace to the grave.

"O, I remember him well. He went down with the lugger in the Ægean Sea."

"Nay, father, it was thought so, but he was miraculously saved."

"Does he live?" asked the sultan. "I would see him, for I love him well, and he loved me truly, Esmah, until that time."

"He does live, father, and is the husband of thy child!"

"God is great," ejaculated the sultan. "Arasilus, king of Greece, our former slave?"

"The same, father, but he was of gentle blood, and fortune saved him from the wreck to inherit his right by birth to the throne."

"The ways of Allah are wonderful," said the sultan, musing, while he turned to look upon the face of a sweet and beautiful child that played about the cushioned floor.

"Now I look again upon the boy, Esmah, I see Alick once more—recall his noble face, as he sat with us and sang those songs, and told old legends of his native land. It is strange I never noticed this before. Come hither, my child," he continued, addressing the little boy.

"What do you want, grandpapa?" said the boy, approaching his side.

"To kiss thee, my boy, that's all," said the sultan.

"There are two for you," he replied, playfully kissing twice.

"You are prodigal of them, my boy."

"O, I have any quantity for you, grandpapa."

"This is a strange story, Esmah, that is told in thy love and marriage; and strange that I should never have suspected the truth. You loved the page, then, when he was thy father's slave?"

"Loved him, father? He was all in all to me, even as now!" said Esmah.

"I do remember how sad thou wert when he was gone, and we thought thee ill. But all is clear again, and I am content, so that thou art happy, my child."

"My own dear father!" said Esmah, kissing his high and noble forehead.

"You go again to-morrow, my child, to join your husband at Athens?"

"Yes, father."

"I am growing old, my child," said the monarch, sympathetically.

"I know it, father, and I grieve to leave thee at such a time."

"It is not that I refer to; but it is well to understand ourselves, Esmah. I may not see thee or thy husband again this side of paradise, where Allah grant we may all meet. Tell Alick I

loved him well, and that you told me all; tell him he must ever
love and cherish thee, not only for thy own sake, but for mine
and this noble boy's. So now, my child, farewell!"

The sultan was indeed gradually descending to the last resting-place of his people, and ere Esmah had fairly reached her
home at Athens, he was laid in state at St. Sophie, while his
son rose at once to fill the throne so long occupied by the
father.

Arsilus, king of Greece, reigned peacefully and happily for
many years at Athens, and left, as tokens of his liberality and
taste, many a classic remembrance and kingly endowment.

PRICE REDUCED.—We are happy to announce that,
with the next issue of TEN CENT NOVELETTES, the old price,
ten cents per copy, will be resumed. It was with the greatest
reluctance that we raised the price, but circumstances forced
us to do so. We now take great pleasure in being able to
return to the old rates; and in assuring those who have stood
by us through the past ten months, that we shall endeavor in
the future to give them the full value for their money, as we
believe we have done in the past.

The next issue, No. 22, will consist of a powerful and thrilling
Novelette, written expressly for us, by JANE G. AUSTIN, en-
titled, "THE NOVICE: or, MOTHER CHURCH THWARTED."
This is the most singular and remarkable story ever published
by us, and will hold the reader's closest attention to the end.
We published a story by the same author in the "Monthly
Novelette" some six months since, entitled "KINAH'S CURSE,"
which is having an enormous sale, and attracts more attention
than any work we have published for years. Remember that
No. 22 will be but *ten cents per copy*.

BATTLING THE WATCH.

As the world goes, Captain Thayer, of the comfortable, eastern built, New York owned ship Lamplighter, was a Christian. He believed nothing in fighting a crew into discipline, cursing ropes' ends into running bowlines, and making quarter decks prize rings. Moral suasion was his rule, and in the abstract it worked most admirably. But Captain Thayer had one weakness that indirectly affected the comfort always of one or two, and sometimes more of his crew, on every voyage.

Captain Thayer's owners were aware of this infirmity, but it was a delicate subject to broach, one that really was none of their business to meddle with authoritatively, and so the captain continued year after year in command of the ship, without ever having been reminded, or probably aware of his objectionable habit. What the habit was, will perhaps best appear in an account of the manner in which he was cured of it.

The ship had been for a good while a regular cotton carrier, going out from New Orleans to Havre, thence to New York and back to New Orleans—so going the rounds.

Once, in Havre, Captain Thayer received a letter from his owners, informing him that the ship, or the controlling part of her, had been sold, and it was possible the owner might take a fancy to put some other captain in her, in which case they would either buy or build him another ship. Upon his arrival in New York, however, there was nothing said about a change of masters. All Captain Thayer heard was, that the party who had purchased the controlling interest wished him to continue in command, and he did not even know who his new owner was.

Captain Thayer had an off-hand fashion of shipping his officers, and wanting a chief mate on this particular voyage, he shipped him in what he called his "off-hand way," which was just this:

Seeing a keen, wide-awake, well dressed young man standing on the wharf, looking quietly at the ship, Captain Thayer walked up to him and began to ship him "off-hand."

" Do you want a berth, sir ?"

" Yes, sir, I am looking for a ship."

" Well, sir, there's a good ship, bound to New Orleans, thence to Havre and home here again. Good round voyage, sir. I want a chief mate, and you can have the berth. I'll give you the highest wages out of port."

" Thank you, sir; but I am a stranger to you. I can refer you, however, to those—"

" O, nonsense, Mr.—ah—a—what is your name ?"

" John Lisle, sir."

" Well, Mr. Lisle, I don't care a fig for references. I never look at 'em. My eyes are my guide, sir. I can look right through a man and read him like a nautical almanac. I never make a mistake, Mr. Lisle. You'll suit, sir. When can you come aboard, sir ?"

" In half an hour."

" Very well, I like that. We pay a month's advance, and I'll bring it down to you to-morrow."

" There is no occasion, captain. I never take any advance."

" Indeed ! That's singular, but that's another good recommendation. I never make mistakes in my men, sir. Now I have a second mate aboard there that's been with me six years. I should take him for chief mate, only he can neither read nor write. A good man, sir; capital good second mate Mr. Riper is. I never make a mistake in my men, Mr. Lisle."

It is not likely that Captain Thayer had any idea of uttering a falsehood in that assertion, but the truth is he had made a most egregious mistake in Mr. Lisle. Not in regard to his qualification as first officer of his ship, for Jack Lisle never had a superior in that capacity. But if Captain Thayer had known but a thousandth part about the man the day he shipped him as he did before he got to Havre, he would have had some other man in his place if one was to have been found in six seaports; or, failing in that, he would sooner have stood his own watch the round voyage than had Jack Lisle with him as chief mate. He used to make that declaration often afterwards.

Mr. Lisle found the second mate of the ship a great burly giant of a fellow—a sulky, silent Schleswig-Holsteiner, whose English was but half intelligible; and before he had been an hour in the ship, he learned from the second dickey's treatment of two apprentice boys, that he was a tyrant, and an ignorant, brutal one at that.

During the first week of the passage to New Orleans Mr. Lisle discovered Captain Thayer's weakness. It was indulgence of that lignumvitæ-headed beast of a second mate in his acts of petty tyranny towards two or three of the crew whom the fellow had selected out to vent his unmanly spite upon. The eldest of the apprentices informed Mr. Lisle that such was always the fellow's practice, and a dog's life his victims had of it so long as they remained in the ship.

Mr. Lisle argued that as it was but a short run to New Orleans, and the crew would all leave the ship there, it was scarcely worth while to attempt a reform then, but he said to himself, decidedly:

"If I don't teach that double-headed Dutchman that every Jack is a *man*, so long as he behaves himself, before we get to Havre. I'm not Jack Lisle, that's all."

During the time the ship remained in New Orleans matters went on rather quietly. Riper was a first-class sailor man, and he knew it. Nevertheless, Mr. Lisle had an eye on him in everything, and the Dutchman knew that too, and it galled him; but he couldn't well help himself. Mr. Lisle was as good a sailor as himself, and gave his orders in a quiet way, that said plainly enough, "you had better obey, sir."

In a week or so after the ship got to sea Riper had got well settled down into his habitual objectionable practice of tyranny, having selected as his subjects two men who, for all that the mate could discover, were as good sailors and every way as well behaved men as there were in the ship. Mr. Lisle mentioned the circumstances two or three times to Captain Thayer, who only laughed at the mate's remonstrance, saying always:

"O, Mr. Riper is a good man—a capital man. Mr. Lisle, I never make mistakes, sir."

"But you do make a mistake—a very great mistake, sir," remonstrated Mr. Lisle. "You indulge and encourage Mr. Riper in this reprehensible practice. All men whose conduct entitle them to it, ought to receive like good treatment. But they don't here, sir. You know that as well as I do."

"I acknowledge I do know it, Mr. Lisle, and that it is wrong. But I can't help it, sir."

"Then I can, Captain Thayer, and it were better that you warn your pet that such is my intention."

That same day Mr. Lisle observed that the captain held a long and, it seemed, very confidential conversation with the

second mate, and though he believed that the captain had repeated all that had passed between them, the fellow's changed
manner, sullen insolence towards himself, and redoubled bru-
tality towards his forecastle victims, induced the opinion that
the captain had rather encouraged the man than cautioned him
to mend his manners.

Thus matters went on for a week or so longer, until one
morning, when it was blowing a swinging gale, the ship was
rattling it off dead before it under double-reefed topsails and
fore course, Riper sent Willie Wescott, the oldest apprentice,
then a lad of eighteen, and a prime sailor, aloft just as the bell
struck seven, to perform some service that would occupy him a
full half hour. The boy went without a word, though he was
in the mate's watch, and Riper had no more right to order him
aloft than he had to send Mr. Lisle himself up there. But the
fellow had an especial spite against Willie; besides it was
evident that he was ready that morning to contest the mate's
supreme authority by an appeal to physical force. Mr. Lisle
read it all clearly enough, and himself decided that it was quite
time the Dutchman should be educated as to who was first-
officer of the ship Lamplighter.

Eight bells had been struck and the watch relieved before
Willie finished his job, and when he came down, of course he
was entitled to go down to his breakfast and to his forenoon
below as well as the rest of the watch. But Riper met him at
the foot of the poop ladder, put a tar bucket into his hand, and
ordered him away out on to the flying jibboom to give the guys
a lick of tar; while at the same time there were half a dozen men
of the starboard watch lounging about decks doing nothing.

Mr. Lisle went down the poop-ladder, took the bucket from
Willie, gave it a swing overboard, and then without looking at
the second mate, he said very quietly :

" Willie, go below and get your breakfast !"

The lad made one step, and at the next the great brawny paw
of the brute Schleswiger was grappling his throat. It was but
a single instant, however, for at the next there came a *whell*
from Jack Lisle's fist that slewed the big Dutchman's nose hard
to port, stove in four or five of his front teeth, and drove his
lignumvitæ head against the stern of the long boat like a paver's
rammer.

In a second the hunt was up, and two muscular fellows of the
starboard watch—especially pets of Riper's—set upon the mate

both at once. Never did two men make a wilder blunder. With a kick like that of ten jackasses consolidated, Lisle doubled up one of the rascals like a wet swab, laying him out on top of the second mate. The other one he gave a *bliff* in the mouth with the flat of his hand that drove the fellow's teeth chock through his lips, and sent him spinning around like a buzz, until finally away he went head foremost *whick* against the bulwarks, knocking the little sense he had in his sconce out of it for a time.

Three or four more of the watch, who were all Riper men, went into the fight directly. But they went out again quicker than they went in, with cut lips, black eyes, and bloody noses; and then Jack Lisle, having fairly warmed himself up to the work, thought it just as well to thrash the whole watch while he was about it, which he did so effectually that he had every soul of them, except the man at the wheel, down at one time, and such of them as had the power of speech left were roaring like bull calves for mercy.

Having settled everything and everybody on the maindeck to his satisfaction, Mr. Lisle went aft, looked hard at the man at the helm, as much as to say, "Look out old fellow how you cross my hawse," then he made some common place remark about the weather to Captain Thayer, looked pretty sharp at him also, went below, washed the blood from his hands, and turned in for the forenoon.

At the dinner table that day Captain Thayer was unusually sociable, chatting with Mr. Lisle and Mrs. Thayer, who half of her life went to sea with her husband, upon various topics, and then, within ten minutes after they had left the table, while the captain and mate were pacing fore-and-aft the quarter deck, discussing the weather and their cigars, the captain addressed the officer in his usual urbane, smiling manner:

"Mr. Lisle, I have made a mistake. I shall stand my own watch the remainder of the passage. I shall not require your services any longer. I cannot allow such doings in my ship as I have witnessed to-day."

"Very well, Captain Thayer." Mr. Lisle was quite as cool and nonchalant as his commander. "You have the right to put me off duty, sir, and I shall not question it. But wont you please do me the favor to step down into the cabin a moment?"

"Certainly, sir; most certainly." Captain Thayer looked somewhat astonished, but went below with the mate.

The second mate was at the table, making an awkward attempt to stow away his dinner through his damaged mouth, and Mrs. Thayer was enjoying her after-dinner lullaby in her great arm chair, rocked by the waves. Mr. Lisle went into his state-room; but he did not keep the captain waiting long. When he returned to the cabin, he laid the log-book open on the table, pointed to his last entry in it, and remarked:

"Captain Thayer, I have made a memorandum of the circumstance there, and now turn the log-book over to you, as you are to act as chief mate. I have only this to say to you, sir. You have been making a grand mistake all your life; never a greater one than in putting me off duty for simply maintaining my authority over this insolent brute tyrant of yours. In conclusion, Captain Thayer, you will leave the ship, sir, as soon as convenient after our arrival in Havre."

"Why—Mr. Lisle—what—what do you mean, sir?" stammered the astounded captain.

"Simply this, sir, that such abuse of power and petty tyranny as has been practised in this ship by this ignorant beast, and sanctioned by you, will be no longer tolerated."

"Sir—I declare—really—this is very extraordinary. Will you explain, Mr. Lisle?"

"With pleasure, Captain Thayer. This, I think, will enlighten you."

Mr. Lisle laid out on the table, under the captain's eye, a legal bill of sale duly attested, of twelve-sixteenths of the ship Lamplighter to Captain John Lisle.

"Is that satisfactory, Captain Thayer? Am I to consider myself off duty, sir?"

"Mr.—Captain Lisle, what do you advise? Please suggest, sir," said the captain, submissively.

"I would suggest, sir, that you reinstate me in my command; that we all continue in the ship to the end of the voyage; that there be no more petting, favoritism or bullying; that on the next voyage we find a better man for second mate—I recommend the lad Willie for the berth. And as for you Mr. Riper, I advise you to go square by the lifts and braces, and keep your weather eye open while Jack Lisle is chief-mate of the Lamplighter."

Order and impartiality ruled in the ship the remainder of the voyage, and when she went to sea on the next one, Willie Wescott went out second mate of her.

FOURTEEN DAY USE

RETURN TO DESK FROM WHICH BORROWED

This book is due on the last date stamped below, **or** on the date to which renewed.

Renewed books are subject to immediate recall.

Lightning Source UK Ltd.
Milton Keynes UK
UKHW020635110520
363086UK00012B/851